EVALUATION OF
WORKPLACE DISABILITY

BEST PRACTICES IN FORENSIC MENTAL HEALTH ASSESSMENT

Series Editors

Thomas Grisso, Alan M. Goldstein, and Kirk Heilbrun

Series Advisory Board

Paul Appelbaum, Richard Bonnie, and John Monahan

Titles in the Series

Foundations of Forensic Mental Health Assessment, *Kirk Heilbrun, Thomas Grisso, and Alan M. Goldstein*

Criminal Titles

Evaluation of Competence to Stand Trial, *Patricia A. Zapf and Ronald Roesch*

Evaluation of Criminal Responsibility, *Ira K. Packer*

Evaluating Capacity to Waive Miranda Rights, *Alan M. Goldstein and Naomi E. Sevin Goldstein*

Evaluation of Sexually Violent Predators, *Philip H. Witt and Mary Alice Conroy*

Evaluation for Risk of Violence in Adults, *Kirk Heilbrun*

Jury Selection, *Margaret Bull Kovera and Brian L. Cutler*

Evaluation for Capital Sentencing, *Mark D. Cunningham*

Evaluating Eyewitness Identification, *Brian L. Cutler and Margaret Bull Kovera*

Civil Titles

Evaluation of Capacity to Consent to Treatment and Research, *Scott Y. H. Kim*

Evaluation for Guardianship, *Eric Y. Drogin and Curtis L. Barrett*

Evaluation for Personal Injury Claims, *Andrew W. Kane and Joel A. Dvoskin*

Evaluation for Civil Commitment, *Debra Pinals and Douglas Mossman*

Evaluation for Harassment and Discrimination Claims, *William Foote and Jane Goodman-Delahunty*

Evaluation of Workplace Disability, *Lisa Drago Piechowski*

Juvenile and Family Titles

Evaluation for Child Custody, *Geri S.W. Fuhrmann*

Evaluation of Juveniles' Competence to Stand Trial, *Ivan Kruh and Thomas Grisso*

Evaluation for Risk of Violence in Juveniles, *Robert Hoge and D.A. Andrews*

Evaluation for Parenting Capacity in Child Protection, *Karen S. Budd, Mary Connell, and Jennifer R. Clark*

Evaluation for Disposition and Transfer of Juvenile Offenders, *Randall T. Salekin*

EVALUATION OF WORKPLACE DISABILITY

LISA DRAGO PIECHOWSKI

OXFORD
UNIVERSITY PRESS

Oxford University Press, Inc., publishes works that further
Oxford University's objective of excellence
in research, scholarship, and education.

Oxford   New York
Auckland   Cape Town   Dar es Salaam   Hong Kong   Karachi
Kuala Lumpur   Madrid   Melbourne   Mexico City   Nairobi
New Delhi   Shanghai   Taipei   Toronto

With offices in
Argentina   Austria   Brazil   Chile   Czech Republic   France   Greece
Guatemala   Hungary   Italy   Japan   Poland   Portugal   Singapore
South Korea   Switzerland   Thailand   Turkey   Ukraine   Vietnam

Published by Oxford University Press, Inc.
198 Madison Avenue, New York, New York 10016
www.oup.com

Oxford is a registered trademark of Oxford University Press

Library of Congress Cataloging-in-Publication Data
Piechowski, Lisa Drago.
Evaluation of workplace disability / Lisa Drago Piechowski.
p. ; cm. — (Best practices in forensic mental health assessment)
Includes bibliographical references and index.
ISBN 978-0-19-534109-6
1. Disability evaluation. 2. Work capacity evaluation. I. Title. II. Series:
Best practices in forensic mental health assessment.
[DNLM: 1. Disability Evaluation. 2. Insurance, Disability. 3. Expert
Testimony—methods. 4. Forensic Psychiatry—methods. 5. Mental
Disorders—diagnosis. 6. Workplace. W 900]
RA1055.5.P54 2011
614'.15—dc22
2010046127

9 8 7 6 5 4 3 2 1

Printed in the United States of America
on acid-free paper

About Best Practices in Forensic Mental Health Assessment

The recent growth of the fields of forensic psychology and forensic psychiatry has created a need for this book series describing best practices in forensic mental health assessment (FMHA). Currently, forensic evaluations are conducted by mental health professionals for a variety of criminal, civil, and juvenile legal questions. The research foundation supporting these assessments has become broader and deeper in recent decades. Consensus has become clearer on the recognition of essential requirements for ethical and professional conduct. In the larger context of the current emphasis on "empirically supported" assessment and intervention in psychiatry and psychology, the specialization of FMHA has advanced sufficiently to justify a series devoted to best practices. Although this series focuses mainly on evaluations conducted by psychologists and psychiatrists, the fundamentals and principles offered also apply to evaluations conducted by clinical social workers, psychiatric nurses, and other mental health professionals.

This series describes "best practice" as empirically supported (when the relevant research is available), legally relevant, and consistent with applicable ethical and professional standards. Authors of the books in this series identify the approaches that seem best, while incorporating what is practical and acknowledging that "best practice" represents a goal the forensic clinician should aspire to, rather than a standard that can always be met. The American Academy of Forensic Psychology assisted the editors in enlisting the consultation of board-certified forensic psychologists specialized in each topic area. Board-certified forensic psychiatrists were also consultants on many of the volumes. Their comments on the manuscripts helped ensure that the methods described in these volumes represent a generally accepted view of best practice.

The series' authors were selected for their specific expertise in a particular area. At the broadest level, however, certain general principles apply to all types of forensic evaluations. Rather than repeat those fundamental principles in every volume, the series offers them in the first volume, *Foundations of Forensic Mental Health Assessment*. Reading the first book, followed by a specific topical book, will provide the reader both the general principles that the specific topic shares with all forensic evaluations, and those that are particular to the specific assessment question.

The specific topics of the 19 books were selected by the series editors as the most important and often-considered areas of forensic assessment conducted by mental health professionals and behavioral scientists. Each of the 19 topical books is organized according to a common template. The authors address the applicable legal context, forensic mental health concepts, and empirical foundations and limits in the "Foundation" part of the book. They then describe preparation for the evaluation, data collection, data interpretation, and report writing and testimony in the "Application" part of the book. This creates a fairly uniform approach to considering these areas across different topics. All authors in this series have attempted to be as concise as possible in addressing best practice in their area. In addition, topical volumes feature elements to make them user-friendly in actual practice. These elements include boxes that highlight especially important information, relevant case law, best-practice guidelines, and cautions against common pitfalls. A glossary of key terms is also provided in each volume.

We hope the series will be useful for different groups of individuals. Practicing forensic clinicians will find succinct, current information relevant to their practice. Those who are in training to specialize in forensic mental health assessment (whether in formal training or in the process of re-specialization) should find helpful the combination of broadly applicable considerations presented in the first volume and the more specific aspects of other volumes in the series. Those who teach and supervise trainees can offer these volumes as a guide for practices to which the trainee can aspire. Researchers and scholars interested in FMHA best practice may find researchable ideas, particularly on topics that have received insufficient research attention to date. Judges and attorneys with questions about FMHA best practice will find these books relevant and concise. Clinical and forensic administrators who run agencies, court clinics, and hospitals in which litigants are assessed may also use some of the books in this series to establish expectations for evaluations performed by professionals in their agencies.

We also anticipate that the 19 specific books in this series will serve as reference works that help courts and attorneys evaluate the quality of forensic mental health professionals' evaluations. A word of caution is in order, however. These volumes focus on best practice, not what is *minimally* acceptable legally or ethically. Courts involved in malpractice litigation, or ethics committees or licensure boards considering complaints, should not expect that materials describing best practice easily or necessarily apply to the minimally acceptable professional conduct that is typically at issue in such proceedings.

This book focuses on the forensic evaluation of disability issues. The nature and legal meaning of "disability" are discussed, along with relevant scientific evidence and the practice literature. Important legal cases and ethical considerations are also reviewed. The book offers a careful description of the role of the evaluating forensic clinician in such cases. Psychological tests and specialized measures that can contribute to these evaluations are incorporated into this description. The interpretation of results from numerous sources of data is always challenging; Piechowski offers a clear account of such interpretation in the context of forensic disability evaluations. Finally, the communication of results in the form of the report and possible testimony is considered.

Kirk Heilbrun
Alan M. Goldstein
Thomas Grisso

Acknowledgments

I have been very fortunate to have the support and guidance of some exceptionally bright, knowledgeable, and generous colleagues, without whom this book would have never become a reality. I would especially like to thank my very patient editor, Kirk Heilbrun, who provided just the right mix of encouragement and prodding to see me through this project, and David Vore, for reviewing the manuscript and graciously sharing his considerable expertise in disability assessment with me. I would like to thank Jeff Green, who was instrumental in introducing me to the field of disability assessment and who for many years has been a great friend and colleague. A very special thank you goes to Alan Goldstein, who not only served as a second editor on this book, but has been a huge source of support, mentoring, and encouragement to me on this project and throughout my career as a forensic psychologist.

Finally, I would like to thank my husband and best friend, Bill, who for more than thirty years has been unwaveringly supportive, patient, and encouraging; and our daughters, Dana and Darcie, who are a constant source of joy and inspiration.

Contents

FOUNDATION

The Legal Context | 1

The term "*disability*" has a variety of meanings, both clinical and legal. Likewise, being designated as "disabled" has important implications for the individual in terms of entitlement to benefits, conferring legally protected rights, securing educational opportunities, or, conversely, in limiting the individual's access to certain activities or pursuits. Given the potential consequences emanating from this designation, forensic mental health evaluators are often asked to assist ultimate decision makers in the determination of disability status. This may occur in the context of employment rights (e.g., Americans with Disabilities Act), educational access (e.g., Individuals with Disabilities Education Act), or entitlement to monetary compensation resulting from an inability to work. This volume will focus on the evaluation of disability with respect to the latter context: the determination of an individual's eligibility to receive disability insurance benefits.

Sociolegal Purpose and History

The purpose of occupational disability insurance is to provide replacement income to an individual who is unable to work as the result of an illness or injury. "Disability," used in this context, is a legal rather than a psychological or medical term. Its definition is determined by the terms of the policy, contract, or program under which the claimant has applied for benefits. Disability benefits may be sought from a number of different sources, depending on the circumstances of the claimant. These sources include private disability insurance policies, public- and private-sector employee benefits, federal entitlement programs, and worker's compensation.

INFO

In order to collect benefits, claimants must meet the disability criteria set by the policy, program, or contract under which they are seeking compensation.

To be eligible for benefits, the claimant must meet the specific definition of disability determined by the policy or program under which benefits are sought. Although this volume will focus primarily on evaluations for private disability insurance benefits, the general concepts discussed apply to disability evaluations of any type.

Regardless of the source of benefits, disability is determined by *functional capacity*, not diagnosis. "Functional capacity" has been described as "that which a person knows, understands, believes, or can do." (Grisso, 2003, p. 39). It is defined by the demands of the context and the role the individual is required to fill in that context. In terms of occupational disability, "functional capacity" refers to the claimant's ability to perform the important duties of his or her job.

Private Disability Insurance

A disability insurance policy is a contract between the policyholder and the insurance company. In exchange for premiums paid by the policyholder, the insurance company agrees to provide a monetary benefit in the event that the insured party becomes disabled as defined under the terms of the policy. Although policies differ, a common definition of disability includes the inability to perform the

INFO

There are several sources of disability income protection, including *individual disability insurance*, Social Security, employer-sponsored coverage, and worker's compensation.

substantial and material duties of one's own occupation due to sickness or injury that occurs while the policy is in effect. Thus, a valid disability claim requires both the substantiation of the presence of a condition as well as proof that this condition creates *impairment* in the functional abilities of the claimant to perform his or her occupation. The cause of the disability, however, need not have resulted from the claimant's employment.

The first disability clause appeared in an American life insurance policy in 1896 (Thurman, 1938). It was eight years before a second company issued disability coverage, joined by seven more companies during the next two years. Over the next five years this trend continued, with 150 insurance companies offering some form of disability benefits. By 1928, virtually every insurance company in the United States offered disability benefits (Thurman, 1938). Although the wording of disability clauses has changed over time, as with modern disability insurance policies, these early clauses provided for the payment of monetary benefits and a waiver of premiums. This allow the policy to remain in force while relieving the claimant of having to pay premiums during the period of disability.

Insurance companies are obliged to thoroughly investigate all claims. When a policyholder files a claim for disability benefits, the company initiates an evaluation of the claim in order to determine if the policyholder is entitled to benefits. If liability for the claim is accepted by the company, the claim investigation continues on an ongoing basis to determine if, over time, the claimant continues to meet the definition of disability. Thus, the insurance company may initially approve or deny a claim, may continue to pay benefits until the claimant returns to work, or may over the course of the claim, terminate benefits if the company believes the claimant is no longer disabled under the terms of the policy.

A disability insurance policy may be purchased by an individual (often by those who are self-employed) or by an employer to cover a group of workers. A claimant who is denied benefits or whose claim has been terminated can request an appeal of the decision by the company. If this decision is unfavorable to the claimant, the claimant can initiate legal proceedings in the form of a civil action against the company. Individual disability insurance (IDI) is regulated by state law. The state with jurisdiction over these disputes is usually determined by the current residence of the claimant.

Group disability coverage provided as part of an employee's health care benefits is governed by the federal law know as the Employee Retirement Income Security Act of 1974 (ERISA). Thus, in the case of employer-paid benefits, ERISA preempts state law. This preemption was upheld by the U.S. Supreme Court in *Pilot Life Insurance Company v. Dedeaux* (1987), in which the Court held that ERISA supersedes all state laws insofar as they relate to any employee benefit plan. Thus, claimants may not pursue tort or breach of contract actions against the benefit plan on the basis of state law, nor do state consumer protection laws apply.

ERISA establishes a set of administrative procedures that must be followed in the event of a dispute between the claimant and the company. These procedures include specific timelines and an internal appeals process. Only when this process has been exhausted does the claimant have the right to proceed to litigation. ERISA does not expressly provide the right to a jury trial, so these cases are almost always decided by judges in federal district court. The only evidence that can be presented in an ERISA case is the administrative record that was assembled during the appeal process and relied upon by the claims reviewer. There are two standards under which this evidence can be reviewed. The *"arbitrary and capricious standard"* relates to whether the denial of the claim was rational and based on fact or if the denial was an *"abuse of discretion."* Alternatively, a *"de novo standard"* may be applied. When the latter standard is used, the court sets aside the original decision and makes its own decision based on a fresh review of the evidence.

The U.S. Supreme Court in *Firestone Tire & Rubber Company v. Bruch* (1989) ruled that the "de novo" standard must be used unless the benefit plan documents specifically granted the plan administrator discretion to interpret the plan eligibility for benefits. Subsequently, in *Metropolitan Life Insurance Company et al. v. Glenn* (2008), the Court affirmed the principles set out in *Firestone* in determining the appropriate standard of judicial review. The *Glenn* Court also addressed the conflict of interest that exists when the benefit administrator (i.e., the entity that decides the claim)

CASE LAW

Firestone Tire & Rubber Company v. Bruch (1989)

● Established the *de novo* review as the appropriate standard for reviewing denial of benefits under ERISA unless the policy specifically gives the plan administrator the "discretion" to determine eligibility for benefits.

also funds the plan's benefits. The Court ruled that this conflict of interest must be considered in the court's review of claim denials.

Social Security Disability

Social Security disability is regulated by a vast body of law consisting of statutory law, regulatory law, rulings, and court decisions. As described in the Social Security Act (42 U.S.C. § 423) and the Code of Federal Regulations (20 C.F.R. §§ 404.1500-404.1599), determination of disability follows a prescribed evaluation process. The use of this process was upheld by the U.S. Supreme Court in decisions including *Heckler v. Campbell* (1983) and *Bowen v. Yuckert* (1987). The first step in this process is to determine if the claimant is continuing to work in a substantial gainful activity. The second step concerns the severity of the claimant's impairments. Third, it must be determined if the claimant's impairments are listed in the regulations. Fourth, it must be

CASE LAW

Heckler v. Campbell (1983) and *Bowen v. Yuckert* (1987)

● In both cases, the U.S. Supreme Court upheld the prescribed evaluation process used to determine disability under Social Security.

decided whether the claimant is capable of engaging in the type of work he or she did in the past. Fifth, it must be determined if the claimant has the capacity to perform other work available in the national economy.

In terms of mental disorders, the Social Security Administration (SSA) recognizes nine diagnostic categories (see Table 1.1): organic mental

INFO

The following five-step evaluation process is used to determine a claimant's eligibility for Social Security benefits.

1. Substantial gainful activity

2. Severity

3. Listed impairments

4. Relevant past work

5. Capacity to perform other work available in the national economy

disorders; schizophrenic, paranoid, and other psychotic disorders; affective disorders; mental retardation; anxiety-related disorders; somatoform disorders; personality disorders; substance addiction disorders; and autistic disorder and other pervasive developmental disorders. Criteria are provided to substantiate both the presence of the disorder and the associated functional limitations, which include activities of daily living, social functioning, concentration, and episodes of decompensation. These criteria are designed so that an individual with an impairment that meets or is equivalent in severity to the criteria of a listing could not reasonably be expected to engage in gainful activity.

Although substance addiction is listed in the diagnostic categories, Title II of the Social Security Act was amended in 1996 with the passage by Congress of Public Law 104-121, such that Social Security disability benefits were terminated to individuals disabled primarily by drug addiction and alcoholism. Thus, a person with substance addiction is only eligible for benefits if he or she is also disabled due to other medical problems. There must be evidence of behavioral changes or physical changes associated with the regular use of substances that affect the central nervous system. Examples of this include organic mental disorders, depression, anxiety disorders, personality disorders, peripheral neuropathies, liver damage, gastritis, pancreatitis, and seizures.

While the overall administration of the Social Security program lies with the SSA, disability determinations are made by state agencies operating under federal law. *Social Security disability benefits* are provided to disabled workers who meet the program's definition of disability, have been disabled for at least five months,

Table 1.1 Social Security Disability Listed Impairments, Mental Disorders—Adults

Category	Description
Organic Mental Disorders	Psychological or behavioral abnormalities associated with a dysfunction of the brain. History and physical examination or laboratory tests demonstrate the presence of a specific organic factor judged to be etiologically related to the abnormal mental state and loss of previously acquired functional abilities.
Schizophrenic, Paranoid, and Other Psychotic Disorders	Characterized by the onset of psychotic features with deterioration from a previous level of functioning.
Affective Disorders	Characterized by a disturbance of mood, accompanied by a full or partial manic or depressive syndrome. "Mood" refers to a prolonged emotion that colors the whole psychic life; it generally involves either depression or elation.
Mental Retardation	"Mental retardation" refers to significantly sub-average general intellectual functioning with deficits in adaptive functioning initially manifested during the developmental period; i.e., the evidence demonstrates or supports onset of the impairment before age 22.
Anxiety-Related Disorders	Anxiety is either the predominant disturbance or it is experienced if the individual attempts to master symptoms; for example, confronting the dreaded object or situation in a phobic disorder, or resisting the obsessions or compulsions in obsessive-compulsive disorders.
Somatoform Disorders	Physical symptoms for which there are no demonstrable organic findings or known physiological mechanisms.
Personality Disorders	Exist when personality traits are inflexible and maladaptive and cause either significant impairment in social or occupational functioning, or subjective distress. Characteristic features are typical of the individual's long-term functioning and are not limited to discrete episodes of illness.

(Continued)

Substance Addiction Disorders	Behavioral changes or physical changes associated with the regular use of substances that affect the central nervous system.
Autistic Disorder and Other Pervasive Developmental Disorders	Characterized by qualitative deficits in the development of reciprocal social interaction, in the development of verbal and nonverbal communication skills, and in imaginative activity. Often, there is a markedly restricted repertoire of activities and interests, which frequently are stereotyped and repetitive.

Source: Social Security Administration Disability Evaluation Under Social Security (Blue Book—June 2006).

are below retirement age, and have filed an application for disability benefits. The Social Security Act's definition of disability requires the claimant to show a medically determinable physical or mental impairment that must be expected to result in death or to last for at least 12 months. The burden of proof of disability rests on the claimant.

Once a claimant is determined to be disabled, termination of benefits on the grounds that the person is no longer disabled must rest on affirmative evidence that the individual's condition has improved. The burden of proof for termination of benefits rests with the state agency. Appeals of determinations are decided by federal administrative law judges and the federal courts.

It is important to note that the federal government uses multiple definitions of disability depending on the purpose or program in question. The Social Security definition of disability should not be confused with the criteria for disability determination under nondiscrimination laws, such as the Americans with Disabilities Act (ADA). Under ADA, a determination of disability requires the presence of a physical or mental impairment that substantially limits one or more "major life activities," the existence of a record of such impairment, or evidence that the individual is regarded as having such impairment. In contrast to this, to be disabled for the purpose of receiving Social Security disability benefits, individuals must have a severe disability (or combination of disabilities) that has lasted, or is expected to last, at least 12 months or result in death, and which prevents working at a "substantial gainful activity" level.

Worker's Compensation

Worker's compensation has been described as more a legal than a medical process (Glass, 2004). In the United States, worker's compensation laws were first enacted in the early twentieth century, beginning with the Federal Employers Liability Act in 1908. This law covered railroad workers and federal employees engaged in hazardous occupations. Individual states, beginning with Wisconsin in 1911, followed suit by enacting statutory systems for compensating injured workers.

Worker's compensation differs from other kinds of disability benefits in that the causation of the illness or injury is a critical factor. The purpose of worker's compensation is to provide for workers who become ill or are injured on the job. Worker's compensation is a "no fault" system intended to reduce the need for litigation. The employee is not required to demonstrate negligence by the employer in order to be eligible for benefits. The employer is immune from tort action by the employee. Benefits are fixed and limited by statute, and include medical treatment and compensation for lost wages. Worker's compensation benefits are handled differently in each state and are governed by statutes, case law, and administrative practices.

Worker's compensation was developed with the intention of compensating for physical injuries. Compensation for mental impairments has been more controversial (Parry & Drogin, 2007). Claims involving emotional stress are categorized as: (1) *physical-mental*, (2) *mental-physical*, or (3) *mental-mental* (Barth, 1990). "Physical-mental" claims, referring to psychological problems arising from a physical illness or injury, are compensable in every state. An example of this would be an employee who develops disabling depression after losing an arm in a workplace accident. "Mental-physical" claims describe a physical condition caused by psychological stress arising in the course of employment. Examples of physical conditions alleged to be triggered or exacerbated by stress include gastrointestinal disorders and cardiovascular disease.

Mental-physical claims are less straightforward in terms of determining causality, due to the difficulty of establishing the causal connection between the emotional stressor and the physical condition. For instance, it may be difficult to prove that the claimant's heart attack was *caused* by a stressful work environment. "Mental-mental" claims refer to mental injuries arising from employment in the absence of a physical injury. Such injuries may stem from a single traumatic event (a robbery at gunpoint), ongoing severe stressors in certain demanding occupations (e.g., emergency medical technicians), or chronic work stress of a more common nature (e.g., being regularly criticized by one's supervisor). Some states stipulate that the stressful event or circumstances must be unusual (Glass, 2004). Few states compensate workers for purely mental injuries when the condition was not the result of an abnormal work environment.

Claims for worker's compensation benefits may be contested by the employer, and denial of benefits may be appealed by the employee. In most states, worker's compensation disputes are decided by special administrative agencies utilizing administrative law judges. Although these administrative decisions may be appealed to the state court system, the scope for possible litigation of worker's compensation disputes is limited.

The Claim Evaluation Process

The process by which disability claims are evaluated varies by the source of the benefits being sought. Social Security disability claims are decided through a process that is defined by statute, regulations, and case law. The procedure by which private disability insurance claims are evaluated is not set by law, and thus varies among insurance companies. It is possible, however, to provide a generic overview of the process of claims adjudication.

In order to be eligible to receive benefits, the claimant must meet the specific "definition of disability" outlined in the policy. "Disability" is defined by the terms of the policy, contract, or program under which the claimant has applied for benefits. Most definitions of disability include two prongs: (1) the claimant must have sustained an injury or illness that (2) renders him or her unable to perform the *substantial and material duties* of his or her occupation (or in some cases, unable to perform any work at all).

The disability claim is initiated when the claimant notifies the insurance company of his or her intention to file a claim. This notice can be provided either verbally or in writing. The company responds by providing the claimant with a set of forms (i.e., "claim forms") that allow the claimant to detail the nature of his or her condition, treatment, and occupation. The burden of proof is on the claimant to provide "proof of loss,"—that is, evidence supporting the claim for disability. This initial proof of loss typically consists of the completed claim forms, medical records, employment records, and other supporting documentation. Once this information has been provided, the claimant has a legal obligation, within in the limits defined by the policy, to cooperate with the insurance company's efforts to obtain the necessary information to assess the claim on an ongoing basis.

Once the claim has been submitted, the company has an obligation to verify the claimant's eligibility for benefits and to investigate the nature of the claimant's impairment and how it compromises the claimant's ability to perform his or her occupational duties. After the company has made a good-faith effort to obtain the material necessary to make an informed claim decision, this material is analyzed and weighed so that a decision can be reached regarding the payment of the claim.

The claimant's treatment records and input from the treating provider, known as the *attending physician*, are important components in the claim evaluation process. "Attending physician" refers not only to medical doctors, but to other treatment providers as well, including psychologists. The treatment records are reviewed and evaluated by an appropriate professional, acting as a consultant to the insurance company. In the case of mental health claims, psychologists are

INFO

Although definitions can vary depending on the policy, contract, or program, "disability" typically means that the claimant has sustained an injury or illness that renders the claimant unable to perform work duties.

often utilized for this purpose. If the records themselves fail to provide sufficient information to assess the claimant's disability, the company will seek additional information. It should be noted that in Social Security disability, the opinion of the treating physician, if well supported by medical and other substantial evidence, is entitled to be given more weight than other factors, such as the opinions of consultants or examining physicians (i.e., the *treating physician rule*). According to the U.S. Supreme Court decision in *Black & Decker Disability Plan v. Nord* (2003), however, this does not apply to private disability claims.

In some cases, the information obtained in the course of the claim evaluation process may yield insufficient or conflicting data. There may be questions about the nature of the claimant's condition or the extent to which this condition impairs the claimant's ability to perform his or her occupational duties. In the case of a disability claim related to a mental health diagnosis, an *independent medical examination* (IME) may be sought from a licensed psychologist or psychiatrist. The IME provider is independent from both the insurance company and the claimant. An IME is never sought from a treating provider or performed by an employee of the insurance company.

CASE LAW

Black & Decker Disability Plan v. Nord (2003)

● The U.S. Supreme Court ruled that that there is nothing in ERISA that suggests that plan administrators must accord special deference or grant more weight to the opinions of treating physicians.

Litigation of Disability Disputes

Legal remedies available to address disability disputes are determined by the source of benefits. As noted previously, litigation options are statutorily limited in worker's compensation, Social Security disability, and employer-paid benefit cases. Broader alternatives are available in individual disability insurance cases, including suing for punitive damages.

Federal law controls both Social Security disability (Social Security Act) and employer-paid benefits (ERISA), so these cases are litigated in federal court. Worker's compensation cases, however, except those involving federal government employees, are decided by state courts and are controlled by state laws. Legal remedies for all of the above are limited to the initiation of benefits, the reinstatement of terminated benefits, and/or the retroactive payment of past-due benefits.

Individual disability insurance cases are much less straightforward. Federal legislation (the McCarron-Ferguson Act of 1945) gives states the power to regulate the insurance industry without interference from the federal government. Thus, questions regarding definitions of disability and the analysis of the claim are determined by state laws. The state having jurisdiction is typically the state where the policyholder resides. However, when the policyholder and the insurance company are from different states, and the amount in dispute exceeds $75,000, the matter may be removed to federal court (28 U.S.C.A. §1332). In this circumstance, the federal court will consider applicable state law to resolve the dispute, but the Federal Rules of Evidence also apply (as in other federal litigation).

Because state law controls private disability insurance disputes, there is no national law that is applicable, and there are no relevant U.S. Supreme Court cases that address these issues. Lower court decisions are controlling only in the jurisdiction in which they were decided. Cases at the state or appellate levels that are discussed in the following sections can be illustrative of the reasoning courts have applied to these cases, but this case law will not necessarily be applicable in the reader's own jurisdiction.

INFO

Social Security disability and employer-paid benefits are regulated by federal law, and cases are litigated in federal court. Worker's compensation is regulated by state laws and decided in state courts. Private disability insurance is governed by state laws, but cases can be litigated in either state or federal court.

The reader should always check the availability of relevant cases in his or her jurisdiction.

There are two primary causes of action under which litigation involving private disability insurance can proceed: *breach of contract* and *bad faith*. An insurance policy is a contract between the insurance company and the policyholder. When one party to a contract fails to perform in accordance with the provisions of the contract, the other party may initiate litigation asking the court to enforce the terms of the contract. Thus, in the case of a disability insurance policy, if the insurance company denies benefits to a claimant, the claimant may ask the court to determine if the company has breached the terms of the policy, and if so, to order the company to pay the disputed benefits. In breach-of-contract litigation, the court can only enforce the terms of the original contract. In most cases, no additional damages can be awarded, although some states allow the recovery of attorneys' fees. Idaho, for example, allows a court to award reasonable attorneys' fees to a prevailing party in any civil action when justice so requires (Idaho Code §12-121).

Both parties to a contract are required to make a "good-faith" attempt to live up to the terms of the contract. When one party intentionally or maliciously refuses to abide by the terms of a contract, this is considered "bad faith." Under the laws of many states,

Table 1.2 | Disability Disputes: Law and Jurisdiction

	Controlling Law	Court Having Jurisdiction
Social Security Disability	Federal	Federal
Employer-Paid Benefits	Federal	Federal
Worker's Compensation	State	State
Individual Disability Insurance	State	State or Federal

"bad faith" may be a cause of action, either on a statutory basis or as a *tort*. (Defense Research Institute, 2006). A tort occurs when one party owes a duty to another party and is derelict in the performance of that duty, resulting in damage to the other party. In a tort action, the party alleging damages (the plaintiff) seeks relief from the court in the form of compensation for the losses caused by the actions of the other party (defendant). The damage to the plaintiff may have been intentional or due to negligence. In addition to actual monetary losses, the plaintiff may seek additional damages for "pain and suffering" or "punitive damages" to punish the alleged wrongdoer (Abraham, 2000). In terms of disability insurance, bad faith may be alleged when the insurance company fails to adequately or fairly evaluate the claim or engages in conduct such as attempting to intimidate the claimant or providing misleading information to the claimant. When the claimant prevails in a bad-faith action against the insurer, damages may far exceed the actual benefits due under the policy.

An example of bad-faith litigation can be seen in a Ninth Circuit case, *Hangarter v. Provident Life and Accident Insurance Company* (2004). Hangarter, a chiropractor, filed a claim for total disability in 1997 due to a shoulder injury. Benefits were paid for eleven months and then terminated. After the company terminated Hangarter's benefits, it continued to deduct insurance premiums from her bank account until the account was drained, at which point the company cancelled her policy. Hangarter sued the insurance company for breach of contract, breach of the covenant of good faith and fair dealing, and intentional misrepresentation. The jury returned a $7,670,849 verdict in Hangarter's favor, $5 million of which was for punitive damages. Among other things, the court noted that the insurance company exhibited bias by its selection of the doctor to perform the IME, by attempting to influence the doctor's opinion prior to his examination of Hangarter, and by failing to provide the doctor with Hangarter's job description. Specifically, the court noted that the insurance company had used that particular IME provider 19 times from 1995 to 2000, during which time the IME provider had sided with the insurance company in all 19 evaluations. In addition, the insurance company's

CASE LAW

Hangarter v. Provident Life and Accident Insurance Company (2004)

● The insurance company exhibited "bad faith" by choosing a biased IME provider and by trying to influence the IME provider's opinion prior to the evaluation.

medical consultant had written to the IME provider in advance of the evaluation, stating his opinion that there was no basis for Hangarter's total disability claim.

The core question in any disability dispute is whether the claimant meets the definition of disability and is entitled to benefits. Although disability policies and state laws differ, in order to qualify for benefits, the claimant must demonstrate that it is illness or injury that prevents the claimant from performing his or her occupational duties (a *factual disability*). This is to be distinguished from *social disabilities* or *legal disabilities*, in which the claimant's inability to work is the result of circumstantial factors such as incarceration, the loss of a professional license, or adverse publicity.

One of the earliest cases addressing these issues is *Gates v. The Prudential Insurance Company of America* (1934), a New York Appellate Court case. Gates, a dairy farmer, was identified as an asymptomatic typhoid carrier and as such was prohibited from producing or selling milk products by the New York State Commissioner of Health. Gates attempted to find other work, but was shunned by the community and was unable to obtain employment. He filed for disability benefits, but was denied. The court found for Prudential, noting that Gates was not ill or physically disabled. His inability to work was due to the limitations imposed by society.

A number of more recent cases involving the loss of a professional license have been litigated. In a Vermont Supreme Court case, *Massachusetts Mutual Life Insurance Company v. Ouellette* (1992), an optometrist was charged with lewd and lascivious conduct with a minor. He lost his license to practice optometry and was incarcerated. He then filed a claim for total disability benefits, asserting he suffered from the mental disorder *pedophilia*, which prevented him from performing the duties of his occupation. It was noted that Ouellette had suffered from this disorder for more than ten years prior to his arrest, and that he had never sought treatment until after being arrested. Despite the disorder, he had continued to practice optometry until prevented from doing so by the loss of his license and incarceration. The court supported Mass Mutual's denial of Ouellette's claim for benefits. Similar decisions were reached in *Goomar v. Centennial Life Insurance Company* (1994) (physician who claimed visions of astral beings had caused him to sexually molest four female patients); *Grayboyes v. General American Life Insurance Company* (1995) (orthodontist who lost his license and claimed total disability due to frotteurism); and *Massachusetts Mutual Life Insurance Company v. Jefferson* (2002) (psychologist who lost his license after an affair with a former patient, and claimed depression caused him to have the affair).

It should not be inferred from this discussion that the presence of legal or social impediments negates the possibility of a factual disability. Consider, for example, the Ninth Circuit's decision in *Damascus v. Provident Life and Accident Insurance Company* (1996). Damascus, a dentist, had his license to practice placed on probation and later revoked based on mental illness, inappropriate care of patients, negligence, and unprofessional conduct. Provident denied the claim, asserting that Damascus was legally disabled due to the actions of the State Dental Board. The trial court granted Provident's motion for summary judgment, but on appeal, the Ninth Circuit Court reversed and remanded, noting that there was a dispute of fact as to whether the loss of his license was due to Damascus's being mentally incompetent to practice.

Another issue that has been the focus of litigation is determining the occupation of the claimant. As noted previously, "disability" relates to the capacity to perform the duties of one's occupation. Thus, identifying the specific occupation and the associated duties is critical in determining eligibility for benefits. Most policies define "own occupation" as the occupation the claimant was performing at the onset of the disability claim. In *Emerson v. Fireman's Fund* (1981), the Eleventh Circuit court noted, "[W]hen an insured changes occupations, it is his occupation at the time of disability, not at the time the policy went into effect that controls" (p. 1267). Disputes may arise when the claimant's most recent work activities vary from the duties performed at the time the policy was purchased, when the claimant's occupational duties are atypical for the occupation, when the claimant is engaged in more than one occupation, or when the claimant has a particular specialty within an occupation.

The question of specialty versus general occupation was addressed by the U.S. District Court for the Eastern District of Pennsylvania in *Brosnan v. Provident Life & Accident Insurance Company* (1998). Brosnan, an anesthesiologist, was terminated by his practice after alcohol was detected on his breath. Brosnan subsequently obtained inpatient and outpatient treatment for alcoholism, chronic dysthymia, acute depressive episodes, and mild organic brain syndrome. Brosnan claimed he could not return to work in the operating room as an anesthesiologist and filed for disability benefits. Provident argued, among other things, that Brosnan's occupation under the policies was that of a medical doctor, as opposed to an anesthesiologist, and therefore Brosnan was not totally disabled because he was working as general practitioner. The court sided with Brosnan, calling Provident's argument "disingenuous at best," noting, "Occupation, as defined by the policies, is the occupation regularly engaged in at the time the claimant becomes disabled" (p. 7).

Occupational definition was also at issue for the U.S. District Court for the Southern District of Florida in *Berkshire Life Insurance Company v. Adelberg* (1997). Adelberg, a yacht salesman, claimed disability due to a knee injury that left him unable to climb around yachts. He subsequently returned to

CASE LAW

Brosnan v. Provident Life & Accident Insurance Company (1998)

- Addressed the issue of specialty versus general occupation

- The U.S. District Court for the Eastern District of Pennsylvania held that the claimant's occupation, as defined by the policies, was the occupation regularly engaged in at the time the claimant became disabled.

work as freight-space salesman. Berkshire denied his claim, asserting that Adelberg's occupation was that of a "salesman," not a "yacht salesman." The court concluded that, since Adelberg was engaged in the activity or business of selling yachts at the time of his injury, his occupation was that of a yacht salesman.

Disputes may also arise when a claimant has recovered or whose symptoms are in remission, but who remains out of work due to "risk of relapse" or "risk of disability." This is often seen in disability cases related to cardiac conditions and in cases related to substance abuse. In the Third Circuit Court, *Lasser v. Reliance Standard Life Insurance Company* (2003), Lasser, an orthopedic surgeon, sought disability benefits due to a significant cardiac condition after his doctors warned him that the stress of performing surgery could aggravate his condition. The court found for Lasser, noting that, as long as there was a "medically unacceptable risk" of a future heart attack or death, Lasser was entitled to benefits.

In *risk of relapse* cases related to substance abuse, the direction of the court has been less clear (Vore, 2007). A number of "risk of relapse" cases have concerned anesthesiologists who became addicted to the opioid medications utilized in the operating room. In most of these cases, the claimant has successfully completed a course of treatment and has maintained abstinence for an extended period of time. The claimant seeks to extend disability benefits due to fears that relapse would occur if the claimant were to return to the operating room and had access to the substances in question. The insurance company asserts that the claimant's condition is in remission and that there are no active symptoms that impair the claimant's functioning. Courts have tended to base rulings on what is judged to be the imminent risk of relapse of the claimant.

In *Laucks v. Provident Companies* (1997), an anesthesiologist who had maintained abstinence for a period of five years was denied disability benefits when he returned to work as a physician in another specialty. In finding for Provident, the court noted that Laucks evinced no continuing cognitive or motor impairments, and there was no evidence that Laucks was unable to control his addiction, given his five-year abstinence.

In *Holzer v. MBL Life Assurance Corporation* (1999), a different conclusion was reached. Holzer, an anesthesiologist, had a sustained recovery from opioid addiction. He had been advised by his treatment providers, however, not to return to work in anesthesiology, due to risk of relapse. His claim for disability benefits was denied. The court, in denying summary judgment, reasoned that factual issues existed regarding the problems and risks to patients in the operating room, as well as the potential harm to Holzer if he returned to work and relapsed.

Likewise, in *Kupshik v. John Hancock Mutual Life Insurance Company* (2000), the court reasoned that factual issues existed regarding the degree of risk present. Kupshik, an anesthesiologist, was confronted by his colleagues about his suspected drug addiction. Kupshik's hospital privileges were revoked, and he entered treatment. He applied for and received disability benefits. Eleven months later, Kupshik, in recovery from his addiction, attempted to return to work but was rejected by his anesthesiology group. Kupshik's disability benefits were terminated on the basis that he was capable of working in his occupation. Kupshik contended that if he were to return to anesthesiology, there was a very high risk of relapse and possible death. The insurance company argued that Kupshik had sustained a recovery without relapse and that his risk of relapse was not as great as Kupshik claimed. The court concluded that determining the level of risk (a factual matter) was pivotal in establishing whether Kupshik was totally disabled by his addiction.

Conclusion

Disability benefits are intended to provide replacement income to an individual who is unable to work as the result of an illness or injury. "Disability" is a legal term defined by the provisions of the policy, contract, or program under which the claimant applies for benefits. Sources of disability benefits include private disability policies, employer-paid benefits, worker's compensation, and Social Security. Each of these sources is controlled by a different body of law, which delineates, to a greater or lesser extent, the definition of disability, the process of claims evaluation, and the avenues available for dispute resolution.

Forensic Mental Health Concepts

2

The preceding chapter described the legal contours of disability. It was noted that *disability* in this context is defined legally, rather than clinically. Decisions about whether a claimant is entitled to benefits are based on the "definition of disability" as articulated in the relevant policy language, statutes, regulations, and case law. A standard definition of disability refers to "the inability to perform the substantial and material duties of one's occupation due to sickness or injury." Therefore, the ultimate disability decision is based on an assessment of the claimant's work capacity in the context of the applicable legal framework.

It should be clear from this discussion that the forensic mental health evaluator is not able to answer the ultimate issue question: Does the claimant meet the legal definition of disability? Although the evaluator may be able to assess the clinical aspects of the claimant's condition and functional capacity, disability determinations are ultimately legal ones, requiring an analysis of the relevant contract language, statutes, and/or regulations. Such analyses are beyond the ken of the expert. Likewise, the claims adjudicator may lack the information to make this determination without input from the forensic evaluator. Thus, the task for the forensic evaluator is to provide relevant psychological data that will assist the adjudicator in rendering a decision. This information should be related to key components of disability determination and must be communicated in a manner that is useful and understandable to the claims adjudicator.

In order to accomplish this, the evaluation data must be converted from psychological concepts into constructs related to the definition of disability. This linkage between the legal and the clinical aspects of forensic work has been termed "forensic mental health concepts" (Heilbrun, 2001). These concepts form the bridge between the legal definitions of disability and the mental health data that is within the purview of the forensic evaluator. This chapter will describe the forensic mental health concepts relevant to the evaluation of disability and demonstrate how an understanding of these concepts can assist the evaluator in developing a plan for the assessment.

Concepts and Terms

Disability and Work Capacity

The term "disability" has a specific meaning within the context of a disability independent medical examination (IME). Therefore, it is important to use this term in a way that conveys this specific meaning, rather than in a more generic or clinical sense. "Disability" can be distinguished from *work capacity*. "Disability" refers to the legal determination of the claimant's eligibility for disability benefits. On the other hand, "work capacity" refers to the claimant's ability to function in his or her occupation. In the context of a disability evaluation, these terms should not be used interchangeably. Despite its being referred to as a "disability" evaluation, the forensic evaluator is really being asked to assess work capacity.

Work capacity can be conceptualized as the interaction of person variables, job demands, and contextual factors. *Person variables* are factors, both static and dynamic, that are intrinsic to the claimant. Such variables include abilities, skills, aptitude, and knowledge, and the claimant's emotional, cognitive, and interpersonal functioning. In contrast to person variables, *job demands* exist independently of the claimant. Also known as *occupational duties*, these elements are usually listed in a job description. They represent both core job duties (referred to as "substantial and material") and the peripheral tasks involved in performing a particular job. Job demands are static factors and are intrinsic to a specific position or occupation. *Contextual factors* refers to all the other factors that affect an individual's performance in a particular job but are not intrinsic to either the individual or the position. Contextual factors might include the length and difficulty of the commute to work, the personality of the supervisor, financial compensation, relations with coworkers, family problems, legal issues, the economy, and work availability. During the course of the IME, it is important that the evaluator understand the differences between person variables, job demands, and contextual factors and be able to distinguish these factors from one another.

Condition, Symptoms, and Impairment

The claimant's condition in light of an illness or injury is important in a disability determination, but the presence of a DSM-defined mental disorder is not synonymous with a finding of disability. The *Diagnostic and Statistical Manual of Mental Disorders*, fourth edition, text revision (DSM-IV-TR) cautions about its use in nonclinical settings. As described in the Introduction (pp. xxxii–xxxiii), the fit between clinical diagnostic data and legal questions is "imperfect" (DSM-IV-TR, p. xxxii). "It is precisely because impairments, abilities, and disabilities vary widely within each diagnostic category that assignment of a particular diagnosis does not imply a specific level of impairment or disability." (DSM-IV-TR, p. xxxiii). Likewise, Gold and Shuman (2009) noted that the presence of diagnosis does not necessarily imply significant or specific functional impairment; furthermore, functional impairment (when present) does not necessarily result in disability.

With the exception of Social Security disability, there is no agreed-upon listing of diagnoses that are cited as specifically relevant for disability. As described in Chapter 1, the Social Security Administration recognizes nine diagnostic categories: (1) organic mental disorders; (2) schizophrenic, paranoid, and other psychotic disorders; (3) affective disorders; (4) mental retardation; (5) anxiety-related disorders; (6) somatoform disorders; (7) personality disorders; (8) substance addiction disorders; and (9) autistic disorder and other pervasive developmental disorders (SSA, 2006). Diagnoses commonly cited

INFO

The presence of a DSM-classified mental disorder does not necessarily imply disability.

as a basis for disability in private and group disability claims include mood disorders, anxiety disorders, substance-related disorders, and cognitive disorders. Mental retardation, pervasive developmental disorders, and schizophrenia are more frequently seen in Social Security disability claims than in private or employer-paid disability claims. Substance abuse, on the other hand, is not accepted as the sole basis for a disability under SSDI.

Although Axis I disorders are most frequently associated with disability claims, Axis II disorders can also be the basis of a legitimate claim for benefits. Personality disorders are enduring patterns of inner experience and behavior beginning by adolescence or early adulthood. These behavioral patterns have the potential to significantly compromise an individual's functioning in the workplace and other important aspects of life. In addition, the presence of a personality disorder does not preclude the possibility of a comorbid Axis I disorder or the experience of acute distress. In fact, some personality disorders may increase the individual's vulnerability to episodes of depression and anxiety. Borderline personality disorder, for example, is characterized by mood instability and difficulties in maintaining interpersonal relationships, factors that may seriously compromise work functioning. Regardless of the claimant's condition, greater focus should be placed on assessing functioning than on assigning diagnostic labels.

Impairment is a term frequently used in disability assessment. The American Medical Association (2008) has defined "impairment" as a "significant deviation, loss or loss of use of any body structure or body function in an individual with a health condition, disorder, or disease" (p. 5). Impairment is both observable and measurable. It is causally related to a health condition, but it is distinct from symptoms. Leo and Del Regno (2001) noted that a common error made by clinicians is failing to distinguish between subjective symptom report and clinically observed data. Because impairment is defined in terms of a loss of function, the presence of a mental health disorder does not determine the existence or explain the nature of any impairment. Impairment also does not determine work incapacity, as the significance of any impairment in functioning can only be determined in relation to the occupational demands of the claimant.

Occupational Demands, Job Duties, and Functional Abilities

Every job has a distinctive set of core and peripheral occupational duties. *Core duties* are typically listed in an employee's job description. These duties are so vital to the performance of the job that, if they are not performed, the very nature of the job would significantly change. *Peripheral duties*, on the other hand, are duties that may be performed in the course of job, but are not essential. In other words, peripheral duties could be changed or eliminated without altering the meaning of the job itself. As an example, consider the occupation of registered nurse. Registered nurses must be able to assess health problems and needs, develop and implement nursing care plans, maintain medical records, and administer nursing care. These would be regarded as the core occupational duties. Peripheral duties might include activities such as participating in hospital committees.

The concept of functional abilities is critical in disability assessment. Just as job duties form the basis of the occupation, functional abilities can be thought of as the building blocks of job duties. In the example of a registered nurse, consider the job duty "assess health problems and needs." The performance of this duty requires a number of underlying abilities. These would include things like listening attentively, selecting and administering assessment tools, and recording observations. Functional abilities are observable and measurable. Identifying and assessing relevant functional abilities is a central component of a disability evaluation.

Attempts have been made to categorize and describe common functional abilities. The Social Security Administration employs a schema called Residual Functional Capacity (RFC) (SSA, 2006). RFCs are descriptions of work abilities that the claimant retains despite condition-related impairments in functioning. The SSA defines four mental RFCs: understanding and memory, sustained concentration and persistence, social interaction, and adaptation.

Unfortunately, the mental RFCs are of limited usefulness outside of Social Security disability determinations. In particular, the mental RFCs fail to account for the level of skills needed to perform high-level, complex professional occupations.

INFO

Mental Residual Functional Capacities (RFCs) listed by the SSA are:

1. Understanding and memory (e.g., remembering instructions and procedures)

2. Sustained concentration and persistence (e.g., working with or near others without being distracted)

3. Social interaction (e.g., getting along with coworkers)

4. Adaptation (e.g., responding appropriately to changes in the work setting)

The World Health Organization (WHO, 2001) developed the International Classification of Functioning, Disability, and Health (ICF). This was designed as a classification of health and health-related domains and was intended to serve as a framework for measuring health and disability at both individual and population levels. Disability and functioning are viewed as outcomes of interactions between health conditions and contextual factors. Under this classification system, specific mental functions include attention functions, memory functions, psychomotor functions, emotional functions, perceptual functions, thought functions, higher-level cognitive functions, specific mental functions of language, calculation functions, mental function of sequencing complex movements, and experiencing self and time functions.

The U.S. Department of Labor has developed an online resource, the Occupational Information Network (O*NET, accessible at http://online.onetcenter.org/) which is a database and directory of occupational titles, worker competencies, and job requirements and contains information on skills, abilities, knowledge, work activities, and interests associated with various occupations. Within this taxonomy, work activities are classified in four general categories: information input (obtaining information and data necessary to job performance); interacting with others (interactions with persons or supervisory activities);

mental processes (processing, planning, problem-solving, decision-making, and innovating); and work output (physical activities).

For the purpose of a disability IME, work demands can be divided into three broad domains: cognitive demands, interpersonal demands, and emotional demands. *Cognitive demands* include areas such as concentration, memory, comprehension, expression, processing, and problem solving. *Interpersonal demands* involve the ability to engage in appropriate interactions with coworkers, supervisors, and the public. *Emotional demands* focus on areas such as stress tolerance, emotional control, mood stability, and judgment. By examining the job description and related information, the forensic evaluator can determine the demands required to perform the core job duties in question and the level of ability needed to meet these demands. This allows the evaluator to decide how to measure the claimant's functional capacity in each area. This process will be discussed in greater detail in Chapters 4 and 5.

Disability as a Legal Competency

A forensic evaluation differs from a clinical evaluation in important respects (Heilbrun, 2001; Heilbrun et al., 2008; Melton et al., 2007). A clinical evaluation provides information about diagnosis, symptoms, treatment, course, and prognosis. A forensic evaluation expands upon and translates this information into data about "functional capacity." Grisso (2003) has defined *functional capacity* as that which an individual can do or accomplish, as well as the knowledge, understanding, or beliefs that may be necessary for that accomplishment. "Functional capacity" is distinct from psychiatric diagnoses and is shaped by the specific context (situational demands). In an evaluation of disability, the relevant functional capacities are those corresponding to the duties of the claimant's occupation. This distinguishes a disability evaluation from most other types of forensic assessment in which the relevant capacities are listed in statutes or defined by case law. For example, a "competency to stand trial" evaluation assesses the defendant's capacity to understand the proceedings against him and to assist in his defense. In contrast, each disability evaluation assesses a somewhat different set of relevant capacities. The functional capacities necessary to work as a neurosurgeon are not the same as the functional capacities necessary to work as an accountant, a kindergarten teacher, or a police officer. An accountant working in a large national firm may have different job duties than an accountant running her own tax preparation service. A police officer in a small town in Missouri may work very differently than a New York City police officer. Thus, it is impossible to identify a single set of relevant functional capacities that should be assessed in a disability evaluation.

In assessing disability, the forensic evaluator must begin by establishing the existence of a condition and identifying the symptoms and manifestations of this condition that are present in the claimant. The claimant's individual job duties must be determined and translated into measurable functional capacities. This allows the forensic evaluator to provide the claims adjudicator with data relevant to rendering a determination of disability by linking the psychological condition and symptoms to the claimant's capacity to perform his or her occupational duties. These links between condition, symptoms, functional capacity, and occupational duties must be clearly established and logically connected.

Grisso (2003) discussed five components common to almost all legal competencies. Grisso's model has been adapted here to form a framework for understanding the assessment of disability and how it relates to the various concepts previously discussed. Although Grisso postulated five components, the model described here collapses this into four components: functional, causal, interactive, and judgment.

INFO

Four components of legal competencies for assessment of disability:

- Functional component
- Causal component
- Interactive component
- Judgment component

Functional Component

The importance of assessing function has been emphasized throughout this chapter. "Function," however, needs to be understood within a specific context in order to have meaning. As discussed earlier, "function" is distinct from "diagnosis" and refers to what an individual can do or accomplish. The relevant functional abilities depend on the legal question. In the case of a disability evaluation, the competence at issue is defined by the legally determined definition of disability. For example, a definition of disability might refer to the claimant's ability to work in any gainful occupation or to perform the duties of his or her current job. Many functional abilities are "generic," and are necessary for the performance of almost any job (e.g., the ability to follow instructions). However, many jobs also require specific functional abilities beyond these generic requirements (e.g., the performance of complex mathematical calculations). In addition, the particular setting of the job may demand certain functional abilities not required to perform the same job in another setting. Thus, determining the person's relevant functional abilities, both specific and generic, requires an analysis of the unique occupational duties of the claimant being evaluated.

The claimant's diagnosis is not dispositive of his functioning. It is sometimes tempting to assume that the presence of a particular condition is strongly related to a specific level of functioning, but this is not a good assumption. There is no mental disorder that precludes all types of functioning. In addition, two individuals with the same diagnosis might function quite differently. Thus it is more useful for the evaluator to directly observe functional abilities than to rely on inferences based on diagnosis or symptoms. This direct observation and assessment of functioning is an essential element of the IME.

Causal Component

Functional impairments alone are insufficient to inform decision-making about disability status. Deficits in functioning must be causally related to the presence of a mental disorder. This process involves three elements. First, the presence of a valid condition must be established. Second, other explanations for the observed impairments must be ruled out. Third, hypotheses concerning the cause of the functional impairments must be formulated and tested.

INFO

Relating functional impairments to the presence of a mental disorder involves three steps:

1. Establishing the presence of a valid condition
2. Ruling out other explanations for the impairments
3. Formulating and testing hypotheses about the cause of the impairments

The establishment of the existence of a condition requires collecting and analyzing relevant information, and using such data to develop a picture of the claimant's clinical status. This is usually familiar ground for a clinician. Given the context of a forensic evaluation, however, simply accepting the claimant's self-reported symptoms at face value as the basis for a diagnostic formulation would be inappropriate. As will be discussed in greater detail in Chapters 4, 5, and 6, it is critical that the evaluator attempt to obtain information from multiple sources regarding the claimant's reported symptoms. This can be accomplished in a variety of ways: direct observation of the claimant, multiple collateral data sources (including records and third-party interviews), and specific techniques and measures designed to assess the validity of the claimant's self-report.

Even after establishing the existence of a valid condition, it cannot be assumed that this condition is the cause of the claimant's functional deficits. Many other factors, exogenous and endogenous, might explain a decline in work functioning. It is important that the evaluator make accurate causal attributions. Exogenous factors are often referred to as *situational factors* or *circumstantial factors*. Such factors frequently affect an individual's work capacity and productivity. These factors include influences such as economic opportunity, job availability, legal restrictions, and family or personal demands. Factors such as having a long commute or transportation issues, working for a demanding boss, and having uncooperative coworkers also affect work functioning. What these factors have in common is that they are external to the claimant and are independent of the claimant's clinical condition. Even without clinical problems, these factors would continue to affect the claimant's work functioning.

Endogenous factors are often more difficult to separate from condition-related functional deficits. They are internal to the claimant, but independent from the effects of a mental disorder. Personality traits such as conscientiousness and achievement drive, for example, have been associated with work performance (Hurtz & Donovan, 2000). Work performance is also affected by innate aptitude; some people are naturally better at certain jobs than are other people. For example, individuals with superior fine-motor coordination tend to make better surgeons than do people with below-average fine motor skills. Other endogenous factors affecting job performance include job satisfaction, personal preferences, and lifestyle issues.

The final element in the causal component is the formulation and testing of hypotheses regarding the cause[s] of the observed functional deficits. Using information derived from theory and research, the evaluator generates hypotheses about the relationship of observed functional deficits with the presence of a clinical condition. This allows the evaluator to determine the likelihood that an observed functional deficit is the result of an existing clinical condition and not due to unrelated exogenous or endogenous factors. The disability evaluation is designed to test these hypotheses through the selection of pertinent methods and procedures.

Interactive Component

The World Health Organization (2002) noted that two major conceptual models of disability have been proposed: the *medical model*, which views disability as a feature of the person and directly caused by disease; and the *social model*, which postulates that disability is a socially created problem and not an attribute of the individual. WHO proposed an alternative bio-psychosocial model that integrated the medical and social models of disability. In this model, disability is viewed as an outcome of the interactions between health conditions and contextual factors.

This concept forms the basis for understanding the interactive component of disability evaluation. In short, disability can be viewed as an interaction between the functional abilities of the claimant and the demands of the claimant's occupation. When the demands of the job exceed the claimant's functional abilities, the claimant's work capacity would be inadequate. On the other hand, the claimant's work capacity would be adequate if her functional abilities met or exceeded the demands of the job. Gold and Shuman (2009) proposed this as a function of "supply and demand," with "supply" referring to the claimant's functional ability and "demand" to the requirements of the job.

Essentially, the interactive component asks if the claimant's functional capacity is adequate to meet the relevant occupational demands. Functional capacity alone is not sufficient to determine work capacity. Work capacity must be defined in relation to a specified context. This context is delineated by the legal definition of disability, which sets the occupational standard to which the claimant's functional abilities are compared. In some cases, this standard is the claimant's occupation. In other circumstances, the standard might be "any gainful employment."

Once the appropriate standard is determined, the claimant's functional capacity is compared to this standard to determine if a discrepancy exists between his ability and the demands on it. Beyond this broad view, there may be finer contextual elements that affect whether the claimant's functional abilities are adequate to meet his work demands. This might include, for example, the work schedule. An individual with bipolar disorder might have adequate work capacity to perform his job duties when working a regular shift, but might be unable to function if forced to work rotating shifts.

Judgment Component

The judgment component seeks to answer the "ultimate issue" question: is the claimant disabled according to the pertinent legal definition of disability? This determination is based on an interaction of all four components discussed in this section. These are: 1) the claimant's functional capacity; 2) the degree to which her functional incapacity is linked to a clinical condition; 3) the demands of the claimant's occupation; and 4) the legal definition of disability. The evaluator's role is to provide data relevant to addressing these issues, but the evaluator should not endeavor to answer this question.

To summarize, the disability evaluation can be conceptualized as a six-step process (see Figure 2.1). First, the relevant occupational standards are derived from the definition of disability. Next, the claimant's core job duties are broken down into the underlying functional abilities required to perform each duty. Following this, the claimant's functional abilities are assessed and measured. If functional impairments are present, it is determined whether these are caused by a valid illness or injury. The claimant's functional abilities are then compared to the predetermined occupational standard. Finally, a decision regarding the claimant's work capacity is reached by the insurance company.

2
chapter

Linking Legal and Clinical Elements of Disability

As described, the process of disability evaluation flows from the legal definition of disability. The definition is composed of standards, each of which must be met in order for the claimant to be adjudicated as disabled. These standards vary from program to

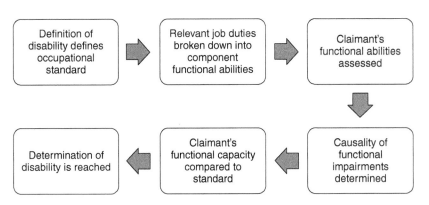

Figure 2.1 The Six-Step Process of a Disability Evaluation

program. The standards for Social Security disability are enumerated in statutory law, regulatory law, rulings, and court decisions. Private individual disability insurance and employer-paid group disability benefits list these standards in the insurance policy. As an example, typical elements of a disability definition include:

- an inability to perform the substantial and material duties of the claimant's occupation;
- the disability must result from an illness or injury;
- the claimant must be under a doctor's care for this illness or injury.

In order to qualify for disability benefits under this definition, the claimant would need to meet each standard enumerated in this definition.

When a forensic disability evaluation is sought, the legal standards must be translated into specific questions that can be addressed by the evaluator. These "referral questions" communicate to the forensic evaluator the specific issues that should be answered through the evaluation. The referral questions should be directly related to the standards in the definition of disability so the claim adjudicator can obtain information from the evaluator that will allow him to reach conclusions regarding the claimant's eligibility for benefits. Given the above definition of disability, referral questions might include:

1. Does the claimant have a valid condition? Is the claimant unable to work because of this condition or for some other reason?
2. Is the claimant able to perform her or his job duties?
3. Is the claimant receiving treatment for the condition causing the impairment?

The forensic evaluator must translate the referral questions into psycho-legal constructs that can be answered through the forensic evaluation by the collection of relevant data and the application of clinical knowledge (see Table 2.1).

Table 2.1 | Psycho-legal Constructs of Disability

Legal Definition	Referral Question	Clinical Knowledge	Data Sources	Psycho-legal Constructs
Disability results from illness or injury	Does the claimant have a valid condition? Is the claimant unable to work because of the condition or for some other reason?	Diagnosis, symptoms, validity of presentation	MSE, clinical interview, psych/neuropsych test results, SVT, review of treatment records, collateral data	Evidence of valid condition. Causal link between condition and functional impairment
Unable to perform substantial and material duties of occupation	Is the claimant able to perform his or her job duties?	Impairment	Psych/neuropsych test results, collateral data, job description	Functional capacity relative to occupational demands
Under a doctor's care	Is the claimant being treated for the condition causing the disability?	Recommended treatments for diagnosis	Review of treatment records	Evidence of participation in treatment, treatment response

Question 1: *Is the claimant able to perform his or her job duties?*

This question pertains to the legal standard "an inability to perform the substantial and material duties of the claimant's occupation." This is related to the clinical concept of "impairment" or the loss of function due to a health condition, disorder, or disease. Since "impairment" is not synonymous with "work incapacity," the evaluator should translate data about impairment to statements about functional capacity. This can then be compared to the demands of the claimant's occupation in order to determine if the claimant's functional capacity is sufficient to meet the demands of her occupation. Information obtained from psychological and neuropsychological testing, collateral data, and the claimant's job description is useful in addressing this issue.

Question 2: *Does the claimant have a valid condition? Is the claimant unable to work because of this condition or for some other reason?*

These questions address the legal standard "The disability must result from an illness or injury" and encompass clinical concepts related to diagnosis, symptoms, and validity of presentation. Responding to these questions requires that the evaluator determine that (1) there is evidence of a valid condition, and (2) a causal link between the condition and the observed functional deficits can be established. Information related to these questions can be obtained from the mental status examination, clinical interview, psychological and neuropsychological test results, symptom validity testing, review of treatment records, and collateral data.

Question 3: *Is the claimant receiving treatment for the condition causing the impairment?*

This question is relevant to the associated legal standard ("The claimant must be under a doctor's care for this illness or injury"). It addresses whether the claimant is under the care of a doctor, but also if this care is directed toward treating the condition in question.

Clinical knowledge and access to relevant research will allow the evaluator to identify appropriate treatments for the claimant's diagnosis. Information about nature and purpose of the claimant's treatment can often be obtained through review of the treatment records or through data obtained directly from the treatment provider. This will allow the evaluator to form an opinion about the claimant's participation in and response to treatment.

Conclusion

This chapter presented forensic mental health concepts related to the evaluation of disability. These concepts form a bridge between the legal and clinical aspects of forensic work, allowing the forensic mental health evaluator to provide data that will assist the claim adjudicator in determining benefit eligibility.

2
chapter

The legally derived definition of disability provides the basis for the disability evaluation by describing the legal competencies at issue. Competencies include functional, causal, interactive, and judgment components. In terms of disability evaluations, these components refer to the claimant's functional abilities and the causal connection between impairments in functioning and the presence of an illness or injury. Disability is understood from a biopsychosocial perspective in which it is viewed as an interaction between the person and situational demands. Accordingly, disability is said to exist when the claimant's functional abilities are insufficient to meet the applicable occupational demands.

To facilitate a forensic mental health evaluation of disability, the legally determined standards are translated into referral questions and presented to the evaluator. Using forensic mental health concepts, the evaluator determines the associated clinical concepts and information sources that will be helpful in responding to these questions. This allows the evaluator to employ clinical knowledge and methodologies to address the psycho-legal issues of the evaluation and to provide this information to the claims adjudicator in a comprehensible manner.

Empirical Foundations and Limits | **3**

This chapter will address the empirical foundations and limitations relevant to disability evaluation. This discussion will focus on three domains. In the first section, information on the prevalence of disability claims and the demographics of disability claimants will be presented. The second section will focus on the relationship between mental health disorders and disability outcomes. Research regarding the impact on work-functioning of various mental health conditions and the effect of treatment will be discussed. The third section will focus on the disability evaluation itself. Research related to the use of psychological tests, self-report data, and third-party information will be presented. This will conclude with a discussion of the prevalence of dissimulation in disability claims and appropriate methods to address this in the evaluation.

Disability Claims and Claimants

What differentiates people with a mental or physical condition who continue to work from those who file a claim for disability benefits? According to the National Health Interview Survey, 16.2 million working-age people (i.e., 10.5% of the population between the ages of 18 and 64) have a work limitation (Stoddard et al., 1998). The Current Population Survey estimated that 34% of work disabilities limit the kind or amount of work that can be done, while 66% of those with work disabilities are unable to work at all (Stoddard et al., 1998). It has been estimated that approximately three-quarters of people with disabilities with no recent work history receive Social Security disability benefits (Johnson & Johnson, 2006).

The five states with the highest percentages of work disabilities are in the South: West Virginia (12.6%), Kentucky (11.4%), Arkansas (11.2%), Mississippi (11%), and Louisiana (10.3%). New Jersey (6.2%), Connecticut (6.4%), Hawaii (6.6%), Alaska (6.6%), and Illinois (6.9%) have the lowest percentages of work disabilities (Stoddard et al., 1998).

The nature as well as the severity of the condition affects work capacity. Employment is lowest for those with limited mobility. Only 22% of individuals using a wheelchair report being employed (Stoddard et al., 1998). Back disorders are the most frequent cause of work limitation, accounting for 21.1% of work disabilities. This is followed by cardiac conditions (10.9%), arthritis (8.3%), and respiratory diseases (5.6%). Mental disorders account for 4.9% of work disabilities (Stoddard et al., 1998).

Education level also affects labor force participation. Among those with work disabilities who are of working age, only 16% of those with less than 12 years of education were in the labor force. Labor force participation rises to 27.3% for those who completed 12 years of school, increases again to 40.9% for those with 13 to 15 years of education, and reaches 50.6% for people with 16 or more years of education (Stoddard et al., 1998). For people with work disabilities, labor force participation generally decreases with age. Almost 39% of 25- to 34-year-olds with work disabilities are employed, versus 18.6% of those 55 to 64 years old (Stoddard et al., 1998).

Some studies have looked at the influence of external factors on claims for disability benefits. Autor and Duggan (2006) related increases in Social Security disability claims to a more liberalized screening process for applicants and, to a lesser extent, to rising financial incentives and changes in labor force participation rates. Kaye (2004) noted that, while claims for disability benefits may increase in difficult economic times, overall health worsened as well. Estroff et al. (1997) noted that impairment and absence of adequate financial and social resources were related to claims for Social Security disability benefits.

Mental Health Disorders and Disability

Mental health disorders have a substantial effect on the health and functioning of the world population. Prince (2007), quoting data from the World Health Organization, reported that neuropsychiatric disorders account for up to a quarter of the burden of worldwide disease and up to a third of the burden attributed to non-communicable diseases. The conditions that are the biggest contributors to this burden are affective disorders (unipolar and bipolar depression), substance-use disorders, schizophrenia, and dementia. In 2005, 40,000 deaths were attributed to mental disorders, especially affective disorders, schizophrenia, and post-traumatic stress disorder. Another 182,000 deaths were attributed to drug and alcohol use. Mental disorders also may exacerbate or be exacerbated by other medical or physical conditions (Prince, 2007).

The National Institute of Mental Health (2001) estimated that 22.1% of Americans ages 18 and older (i.e., about 44.3 million people) suffer from a diagnosable mental disorder in a given year. In 1996, the direct costs of mental health services in the United States were $69 billion—or 7.3% of the total health spending. An additional $12.6 billion was spent on substance-abuse treatment. In 1990, mental illness resulted in a loss of $78.6 billion due to lost productivity as a result of premature death or disability.

Mental illness has a greater effect on disability than on mortality (U.S. Department of Health and Human Services, 1999). Mental disorders were the primary impairment for 25% of the workers awarded disability benefits by the Social Security Administration in 2002 (SSA, 2002). In terms of private disability insurance claims, statistics for

INFO

Mental disorders account for about one-quarter of Social Security disability payments in the United States.

1999 through 2000 indicate that 12.7% of disability claims were due to psychiatric and emotional problems and 3.3% were due to substance abuse (Health Insurance Association of America, 2000). Despite this, Mechanic (2002), using National Health Interview Survey data from 1994 and 1995, noted that about 50% of the population with mental disorders was gainfully employed across a range of occupations. By comparison, the rate of employment was about 76% for the population in general and about 70% for those with a physical condition. The types of occupations performed by those with and without mental illness were quite similar, with the exception of the greater proportion of employees with mental illnesses in the service sector. Among those with mental illness, higher rates of employment were associated with more education and younger age. The presence of mental illness affected income levels as well. Ettner et al. (1997) estimated that the presence of a psychiatric disorder resulted in an 18% reduction in income for women and a 13% reduction for men.

Depression

Major depression is the leading cause of disability in the United States for ages 15 to 44 (NIMH, 2001). It affects almost 10 million American adults each year, and about twice as many women as men. The average age of onset of depression is in the mid-twenties, but it can develop at any age. Dysthymic disorder affects approximately 5.4% of the U.S. adult population, with an age of onset from childhood through early adulthood (NIMH, 2001). The highest lifetime risk was among middle-aged adults (Hasin et al., 2005). Half of those with major depression reported wanting to die, with a third considering suicide and 9% having made a suicide attempt. Current and lifetime major depressive disorder was associated with other psychiatric disorders, especially substance dependence, anxiety disorders, and personality disorders (Hasin et al., 2005).

INFO

Mental health disorders can interfere significantly with vocational performance. Depression, bipolar disorder, anxiety disorders, substance abuse, and cognitive disorders can all have an effect on a person's work capacity.

It has been estimated that as many as 80% of people with depression can be treated effectively, generally without missing much time from work or needing costly hospitalization (U.S. Department of Health & Human Services, 1999). Effective treatments for depression include medication, psychotherapy, or a combination of both. These treatments

usually begin to relieve symptoms in a matter of weeks. Hasin et al. (2005) found that only about 60% of those with major depression received treatment. Women were more likely than men to obtain treatment. The average time between onset of the illness and treatment was about three years. Dewa et al. (2003) found that workers using recommended first-line agents at recommended doses were significantly more likely to return to work than file a claim for long-term disability benefits or leave work.

Depression can have a significant impact on work functioning. Surveys have estimated that between 1.8% and 3.6% of workers in the United States suffer from major depression, and 37% to 48% of these individuals experience short-term disability (Goldberg & Steury, 2001). Depression was associated with a higher rate of short-term work disability than virtually any other chronic condition (Kessler et al., 1999). Depressed workers were found to have between 1.5 and 3.2 more short-term disability days per month than other workers, leading to an average monthly productivity loss of between $182 and $395 (Kessler et al., 1999). Absenteeism among depressed workers was found to be greater among those not receiving treatment and those with more severe symptoms (Souêtre et al., 1997). Early intervention with antidepressant medication was significantly associated with a shortened disability episode (Dewa et al., 2003). A prospective study of Finnish workers with major depression found that long-term disability was predicted by both baseline functioning and duration of depression. Taking sick leave for depression was associated with an increased chance of being granted a disability pension, even after controlling for other factors (Rytsaia et al., 2007).

Specific impairments in occupational functioning related to depression have been identified. A longitudinal study comparing patients with depression to those with rheumatoid arthritis and to healthy individuals found depression-related impairments affected those individuals' performance of mental-interpersonal tasks, time management, output tasks, and physical tasks. These functional deficits persisted even after an improvement in clinical symptoms, such that clinical improvement did not result in full recovery of job performance (Adler et al., 2006). Mildly impaired executive functions were found in another study, including impaired verbal fluency, inhibition, working memory, set-maintenance and set-shifting (Stordal et al., 2004). Depressed persons were found to spend more days in bed than people with chronic medical conditions such as hypertension, diabetes, and arthritis (Wells et al., 1989). Unfortunately, the use of antidepressant medications (specifically SSRIs) was found to be associated with impaired episodic memory and poorer recognition memory (Wadsworth et al., 2005).

In addition to the presence of residual symptoms, it has been hypothesized that return to work can be compromised by other factors, including the development of an "illness identity." This involves the internalization of symptoms as a part of the core identity and justification for remaining out of work (Millward et al., 2005). This illness identity was found to inhibit recovery and return to work. On the other hand, those with depression who were able to dissociate from the illness had better outcomes, despite the fact there was no difference in the severity of depression between these two groups (Millward et al., 2005).

Bipolar Disorder

Bipolar disorder has been described as a chronic, relapsing condition (Tse & Walsh, 2001). Less common than major depression, Bipolar I Disorder has a lifetime prevalence of 3.3% and Bipolar II Disorder has a lifetime prevalence of 1.1% (Hasin et al., 2005). Bipolar disorder affects about 1.2% of American adults each year, affecting both men and women equally (NIMH, 2001). The average age of onset for the first manic episode is in the twenties. According to one study, in addition to episodes of mania, 79.5%

of those diagnosed with bipolar disorder had also experienced at least one clinically significant episode of depression. The most frequent symptoms reported for manic episodes were elevated or irritable mood (95.5%), excessive activity (93.7%), racing thoughts (91.1%) and reduced need for sleep (90.2%). The symptoms most frequently appearing in depressive episodes were dysphoria with anhedonia (79.5%), suicidal ideation (78.6%), loss of energy (68.7%), poor concentration (64.3%), initial insomnia (58.0%), and diminished libido (58.9%). Over 85.7% reported at least one episode of delusional thinking, with the majority of these episodes lasting less than a week (Morgan et al., 2005).

Given this picture, it is unsurprising that individuals with bipolar disorder report difficulty with occupational functioning. Hammen et al. (2000) observed that there is dramatic variability in the work functioning of bipolar patients. Tse and Walsh (2001) noted that employment rates tend to be low compared with that of the general population. They reviewed ten studies examining employment rates of individuals with bipolar disorder, finding employment rates ranging from 27% to 72%.

A number of obstacles to work functioning have been noted in the literature. One qualitative study noted variations in work output due to mood cycling, increased interpersonal conflicts with coworkers, rash decision making, loss of work time, and coping with stigma (Michalak et al., 2007). Another study (Hammen et al., 2000) found that although clinical factors (e.g., recent symptomatology, prior hospitalizations) contributed to overall job functioning, psychosocial factors (e.g., the quality of close relationships) emerged as stronger predictors. Stressful life events were not found to be associated to work adjustment. Kessler et al. (2006) found bipolar disorder was associated with about two and a half times as many lost days from work as was depressive disorder. However, this higher work loss was due to more severe and persistent depressive episodes in those with bipolar disorder rather than to the effects of mania or hypomania.

The effect of cognitive factors on the functioning of individuals with bipolar disorder has been explored in a number of studies. Assessing functioning across manic, hypomanic, depressed, and euthymic states, Martinez-Aran et al. (2004) found that patients with bipolar disorder tended to perform more poorly than normal controls on measures of verbal memory and executive functions. Comparing patients with bipolar disorder in depressed versus euthymic states, Martinez-Aran et al. (2002) found that the depressed group demonstrated poorer verbal fluency. Borkowska and Rybakowski (2001) compared the cognitive functioning of bipolar depressed patients and unipolar depressed patients. The bipolar patients had a higher degree of frontal lobe–related dysfunction than did the unipolar patients. This included poorer visual-spatial and visual-motor abilities. These findings were unrelated to the intensity of the depressive symptoms. MacQueen et al. (2007) found that bipolar patients who had undergone treatment with electroconvulsive therapy (ECT) had greater deficits in aspects of learning and memory than did bipolar patients who had no history of ECT.

Martinez-Aran et al. (2007) looked at how bipolar patients functioned in between active episodes: in others words, they explored the gap between clinical recovery and functional recovery. They found that low-functioning patients had higher levels of cognitive dysfunction, which was independent of illness severity. Lower-functioning patients were found to perform worse on measures of verbal memory and executive function. Thompson et al. (2007) explored the cognitive functioning of bipolar patients during periods of remission, finding deficits in the executive control of working memory—that is, the inability to monitor the contents of working memory. Malhi et al. (2007), following a cohort of subjects, found support for the persistence of cognitive deficits beyond the remission of symptoms, including changes in attention and memory that were correlated with psychosocial functioning.

INFO

Cognitive dysfunction can have a significant effect on work functioning for individuals with bipolar disorder, even during periods of remission.

Anxiety Disorders

Anxiety disorders include, among others, panic disorder, obsessive compulsive disorder (OCD), post-traumatic stress disorder (PTSD), generalized anxiety disorder, and agoraphobia. Taken together, anxiety disorders affect about 13.3% of American adults between the ages of 18 and 54 each year (NIMH, 2001). Anxiety disorders often accompany other mental disorders, including depression, eating disorders, and substance abuse. Women are more likely than men to suffer from anxiety disorders.

Individuals with anxiety disorders, including panic disorder, generalized anxiety disorder, social phobia, and OCD, had significantly higher work disability than control subjects (Kennedy et al., 2002). Panic disorder with agoraphobia was associated with severely impaired work efficacy, primarily related to avoidant behavior (Latas et al., 2004). Specifically, patients reported decreased time spent on work and other activities, reduction in occupational productivity, limited work realization, difficulties in job performance, and a decrease in intense physical activity.

Untreated OCD has been associated with higher rates of unemployment and decreased work productivity (Fireman et al., 2001). Other studies have investigated cognitive dysfunction among patients with OCD. A 2003 review of the literature by Greisberg and McKay found support for the presence of specific executive-functioning deficits and inconsistent findings regarding deficits in memory. Cohen et al. (2003) noted previous support in the literature for information-processing deficits in individuals with OCD. They extended this by investigating the effect of anxiety on selective attention, finding that performance on tasks requiring selective attention substantially deteriorated as anxiety levels increased. Roh et al. (2005) found significantly impaired performances in visuospatial memory, and verbal fluency among patients with OCD even after a year of treatment.

Post-traumatic stress disorder has been studied extensively. According to the DSM-IV-TR, the diagnosis of PTSD requires exposure to a traumatic event in which the person experienced, witnessed, or was confronted with an event or

3
chapter

INFO

Avoidant behavior related to panic disorder has the potential to significantly compromise work functioning.

events that involved actual or threatened death or serious injury, or threat to the physical integrity of the self or others; and that the person's response involved intense fear, helplessness, or horror. It has been estimated that one-third of the population will be exposed to a trauma of this nature at some point in their lives (Brunello, 2001). Among those exposed to such events, most people will not develop PTSD. Brunello et al. (2001) noted that only 10% to 20% of people exposed to severe trauma develop PTSD. In situations involving compensation, however, rates of reported PTSD are significantly higher. Rosen (2004), for example, noted that rates of 86% had been reported in the context of a maritime accident. In the general population, the prevalence of PTSD has been estimated to range from 3% to 6% (Brunello, 2001).

PTSD is twice as common among women as among men (Kessler, 1995). The traumas most commonly associated with PTSD are combat exposure among men and rape and sexual molestation among women (Kessler, 1995). Some differences have been noted in the symptom profiles of men and women with PTSD. Green (2003) found that men were significantly more likely than women to suffer with irritability and to use alcohol to excess. In terms of symptom frequency, over 90% of the subjects of both sexes with PTSD reported experiencing insomnia, anxiety when reminded of the trauma, intrusive thoughts, irritability, and poor concentration. Other frequently reported symptoms (reported by more than 75% of participants) included loss of interest in one's usual activities, recurrent dreams of the trauma, avoidance of places or activities associated with the trauma, and a foreshortened sense of the future. Only 18% of the subjects reported that they were unable to recall parts of the trauma.

Koch et al. (2005), based on a review of the literature, reported that approximately 50% of those suffering from PTSD have a spontaneous remission of symptoms in the first year; however, as many as 10% of those with PTSD stay chronically distressed. Work disability was hypothesized to be related to both symptom severity and social and interpersonal factors. Brunello et al. (2001) noted that the amount of work impairment associated with PTSD is similar to the amount of work impairment associated with depression, but less than that associated with panic disorder. Matthews (2005) identified high levels of depression, reduced time-management ability, and over-concern or anxiety with physical injuries as barriers to work for individuals with PTSD. Brewin et al. (2007) in a meta-analysis found a robust association between PTSD and impaired memory, especially for verbal memory. Taylor et al. (2006) found that PTSD symptoms of re-experiencing, hyperarousal, and depression predicted work impairment. This impairment was hypothesized to be related to interference with work functioning due to decreased concentration and reduced motivation.

Substance Abuse

According to a national survey, 17.8% of the U.S. population will meet the diagnostic criteria for alcohol abuse at some point in their lives. An additional 12.5% will meet the diagnostic criteria for alcohol dependence (Hasin et al., 2007). Less than one-quarter of those with alcohol dependence receive treatment for this condition. Treatment rates for those with alcohol abuse are even lower. There was an average lag time of eight to ten years between the onset of the disorder and entering treatment (Hasin et al., 2007). The average age of onset for alcohol use disorders is 22.5 years, although the risk for incurring an alcohol use disorder is greatest at age 19. Almost three-quarters of those with an alcohol use disorder experience a single episode of illness versus chronic illness episode, while one-quarter average five lifetime episodes (Hasin et al., 2007).

Alcohol abuse and dependence tend to have a negative effect on work functioning. Those with alcohol abuse disorders tend to have lower earnings than other workers. This may be attributed, at least in part, to the fact that those with alcohol use disorders tend to miss more work time (Mullahy & Sindelar, 1993). In addition, Lehman and Bennett (2002) noted that research had found that employee substance use was associated with an increased likelihood of job-related accidents, absenteeism,

INFO

Almost 18% of Americans could be diagnosed with abuse substances at some point in their lives, but few will receive adequate treatment.

tardiness, negative work behaviors, and acts of workplace deviance such as vandalism and theft. Among professionals, other work-related problems were reported. These included being seen intoxicated or with hangover symptoms, complaints from others of forgetfulness, late or incomplete job assignments, a decrease in the quality of their work, and increased conflict with colleagues (Thoreson, 1986).

Alcohol abuse and dependence have been associated with significant cognitive impairments. Harper (2007), for example, found that even uncomplicated alcoholics showed signs of structural changes in the brain and cognitive dysfunction. Duka et al. (2003) found that repeated withdrawal from alcohol was associated with cognitive impairments related to frontal lobe function. Impaired performance on cognitive tasks sensitive to frontal lobe damage was found in those with relatively mild alcoholism compared to social drinkers (Duka et al., 2003).

Work issues become particularly difficult to sort out when the addiction is to a substance present in the claimant's work environment. Such is the case with anesthesiologists who become addicted to anesthetic drugs such as Fentanyl, which is a highly potent opioid analgesic up to 800 times more potent than morphine (Gold et al., 2006). Gold et al. (2006) noted that while only 5.6% of the licensed physicians in Florida are anesthesiologists, nearly 25% of the physicians being followed for substance abuse or addictions practice this specialty. In addition, anesthesiologists account for 75% of the physicians addicted to Fentanyl. As the work of an anesthesiologist requires access to and work with Fentanyl and similar substances, this creates a heightened possibility of relapse.

INFO

Alcohol abuse and dependence can lead to significant cognitive impairments that may be permanent.

Gallegos et al. (1992) found that failure to complete or to continue to participate in a recovery program contributed to relapse. Among those who participate in and complete programs for impaired physicians, recovery rate is generally high. The Missouri Physicians' Health Program, for example, reported a 94% recovery rate (Bohigian et al., 1996).

Cognitive Disorders

Disability evaluations are not often requested for individuals who have sustained well-documented, severe traumatic brain injuries (TBIs), due to the significant degree of overall functional impairment in this population. McCrimmon and Oddy (2006) noted that a wide range of return-to-work rates has been reported in the literature for individuals with moderate to severe brain injury. One estimate suggested that as many as 66% of patients with moderate to severe head injuries are unable to return to their jobs. Disability evaluations are much more often sought for those claiming work dysfunction due to mild traumatic brain injury or post-concussive syndrome.

"Post-concussive syndrome" has been defined as a condition arising after head injury that produces deficits in somatic, psychological, and cognitive functioning (Hall et al., 2005). Complaints reported by patients include headache, dizziness, photophobia, phonophobia, tinnitus, blurred vision, fatigue, altered taste or smell, depression, anxiety, irritability, apathy, emotional lability, decreased concentration, forgetfulness, impaired learning, impaired reasoning, impaired information processing, and impaired memory (Hall et al., 2005). The severity of head injury required to produce a concussion has not been clearly established. Fox et al. (1995) noted that the report of post-concussive symptoms was significantly related to loss of consciousness after a blow, but that simply bumping one's head, having a psychological condition, and being in litigation were also significantly related to reporting these symptoms. Hall et al. (2005) noted that the preponderance of the literature indicates that the majority of people sustaining symptoms of post-concussive syndrome fully recover within three to six months, and only seven to fifteen percent have symptoms lasting more than a year. Individuals who recover quickly are those who experienced only a brief loss of consciousness, had post-traumatic amnesia lasting less than an hour, and a Glasgow Coma Scale score of 15.

INFO

Most people diagnosed with "post-concussive syndrome." Recover fully within three to six months.

Drake et al. (2000) investigated factors related to returning to work following a mild traumatic brain injury among active-duty military personnel, finding that impaired memory and executive functioning presented the greatest obstacles to returning to work. Likewise, O'Connell (2000) found that intelligence and memory variables were related to the return to work. Fraser et al. (2006) found that those able to return to and maintain complex functioning at work tended to be female, had fewer alcohol problems, had sustained less severe injuries, and had significantly better neuropsychological functioning.

Evaluating Disability

Psychological Tests in Disability Evaluations

Psychologists frequently utilize data from psychological or neuropsychological testing when evaluating disability claimants. However, there is no one protocol or approach recommended in the literature for evaluating disability. The selection of appropriate assessment instruments must be made on an individual basis, with consideration given to the nature of the reported disability, the functional capacities required for the claimant's job, and the specific questions posed in the referral.

As described by Heilbrun and colleagues (2002), measures typically employed by psychologists in forensic examinations fall into one of three categories: clinical assessment instruments, which are designed to be used with clinical populations to assist in assessment, diagnosis, and treatment planning; forensically relevant instruments, which are designed to assess constructs that are primarily used in forensic contexts (e.g., measures of response style); and forensic assessment instruments that are specifically designed to directly assess psycholegal constructs or capacities and are, therefore, rarely useful outside of forensic settings (e.g., measures of trial competence). At present, there are no psychometric instruments that directly measure constructs of occupational disability. Thus, evaluations of disability must utilize clinical assessment instruments and forensically relevant instruments.

As with all forensic evaluations, test selection in disability evaluations should be guided by the psychometric properties of the test, as well as with attention to admissibility issues under the relevant legal standard. Heilbrun (1992), for example, suggested selecting tests based on consideration of the following factors: (a) commercial availability and adequate documentation in two sources; (b) a reliability coefficient of .80 or greater; and

INFO

Most disability evaluations utilize a combination of clinical assessment instruments and forensically relevant instruments.

(c) relevance to the legal issue or to the psychological issue underlying the legal issue. Marlowe (1995) suggested the following criteria for test selection in forensic evaluations: (a) support in the literature; (b) having items that address all relevant content domains; (c) standard administration procedures and justified norms; and (d) reasoning that validly links data to conclusions. Kane (2008) suggested that one way to address whether a given test should be used is by considering the frequency with which that test has been utilized in forensic evaluations according to published surveys.

Boccaccini and Brodsky (1999) surveyed 80 psychologists who were members of American Psychological Association Division 12 (Society of Clinical Psychology) and Division 41 (American Psychology-Law Society) regarding tests used in emotional injury cases. The Minnesota Multiphasic Personality Inventory (MMPI) was the most frequently used instrument (used in 89% of emotional injury cases), followed by the Wechsler Adult Intelligence Scale (WAIS) (50%), the Millon Clinical Multiaxial Inventory (MCMI) (39%), the Rorschach (28%), the Brief Symptom Inventory (18%), the Trauma Symptom Inventory (15%), the Symptom Checklist-90 (14%), the Structured Interview of Reported Symptoms (SIRS) (11%), the Personality Assessment Inventory (PAI) (11%), the Halstead-Reitan (7%), and the Thematic Apperception Test (TAT) (3%). An average of 4.83 tests per evaluation was used.

Lally (2003) surveyed 64 psychologists who were board-certified in forensic psychology by the American Board of Professional Psychology (ABPP) about the frequency of their use of various tests and their opinions about the acceptability of test usage in six different areas of forensic practice (mental status at time of offense, risk for violence, risk for sexual violence, competence to stand trial, *Miranda* waiver, and malingering psychopathology). In terms of malingering psychopathology, the following tests were deemed "recommended": MMPI-2 (64%) and the SIRS (58%). "Acceptable" tests were the MMPI-2 (92%), SIRS (89%), WAIS-III (75%), Rey (68%), (PAI) (53%), Validity Indicator Profile (VIP) (53%), and the Halstead-Reitan (51%). Tests considered "unacceptable" were projective drawings (89%), sentence completion (72%), TAT (72%), 16PF (66%), and the Rorschach (55%).

Archer et al. (2006) surveyed 152 psychologists who were board-certified in forensic psychology by ABPP or who were members of APA Division 41 about test usage in forensic evaluations. The most frequently used tests, by category, were the MMPI (multiscale inventories), the Beck Depression Inventory (clinical scales), the Rorschach (unstructured personality tests), the WAIS (cognitive and achievement tests), and the Halstead-Reitan (neuropsychological tests). In terms of instruments used to assess malingering, the SIRS and the Test of Memory Malingering (TOMM) were used most frequently.

Self-Report Data in Disability Evaluations

Obtaining self-reported information from the claimant is an important component of a disability evaluation. Heilbrun (2001) noted that one of the more important distinctions between forensic and therapeutic assessment is the presumed accuracy of the self-report of the examinee. Psychologists have long recognized that self-reported information is subject to both intentional and unintentional distortion. Although usually thought of as the process of shaping responses in the direction of social desirability, self-report bias can influence the way information is recalled and reported so that it more closely fits the claimant's perception of his or her condition and circumstances. In general, there appears to be a tendency in circumstances where financial compensation is at stake for claimants to report better premorbid functioning and poorer current functioning than may be objectively accurate.

BEWARE
In disability cases the possibility of bias in self-reported data must always be considered.

Lees-Haley et al. (1997) investigated response bias in the self-reported history of factors relevant to the assessment of traumatic brain injury, toxic brain injury, and related emotional distress. Utilizing a symptom questionnaire completed by 131 litigating and 315 non-litigating adults, they found that that the litigating group rated their pre-injury functioning as superior and their current functioning as more impaired compared to that of the non-litigating group.

Williams, Lees-Haley, and Djanogly (1999) emphasized the need to take an "investigative" stance with regard to self-report data rather than simply accepting the examinee's report at face value. They suggested that potential financial gain is reinforcing and creates an incentive for patients seeking compensation to produce false or exaggerated symptom reports, factors that are usually not present in patients seeking treatment. They noted that patients pursuing litigation report more intense, frequent, and persistent symptoms than non-litigating patients do, and that litigants are more vulnerable to influences that can intensify and prolong psychological and neuropsychological complaints.

Greiffenstein, Baker, and Johnson-Greene (2002) investigated the concurrence between self-reported and actual scholastic performance in litigating head-injury claimants. They found that both litigants claiming late post-concussive syndrome and litigants with severe closed-head injuries retroactively inflated their scholastic performance to a greater degree than did non-litigating controls. In particular, the late post-concussive syndrome claimants were found to be systematically biased historians. The authors emphasized the importance of verifying self-reported information through collateral information.

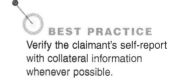

BEST PRACTICE
Verify the claimant's self-report with collateral information whenever possible.

Third-Party Information in Disability Evaluations

The use of third-party data in forensic evaluations is well established (Heilbrun et al., 1994; Melton et al., 1997; Nicholson & Norwood, 2000). Third-party information can take the form of written records or data obtained through interviewing individuals who have direct knowledge of the claimant. Given the potential for bias in the self-report of claimants, third-party information is essential in a disability evaluation in order to develop a more comprehensive and objective understanding of the claimant's condition and functioning. As noted by Heilbrun, Warren, and Picarello (2003), third-party information can "potentially increase the accuracy of findings and conclusions through its integration with other sources of data, as part of a multitrait, multimethod approach to [forensic mental health assessment]" (p. 71). Lewis, Rubin, and Drake (2006) also emphasize the important role of third-party information: "Utilizing multiple sources of data whenever possible is critical in forming a forensic opinion" (p. 43).

Selection of sources of third-party information should be based on an analysis of the potential usefulness of the information in responding to the referral questions of the evaluation and the presumed reliability and credibility of the information. Heilbrun, Warren, and Picarello (2003) note that individuals who have had the greatest degree of contact with the examinee are potentially the most valuable collateral informants. They also caution that it is important to be sensitive to the potential biases of each source. Professionals, as well as family members and friends, can be biased in their views of the examinee. Therapists and other treatment providers, for example, relate to the examinee in a manner that has been described as "supportive, accepting, empathic" as opposed the "neutral, objective, detached" attitude of the forensic evaluator (Greenberg & Shuman, 1997).

Heilbrun, Warren, and Picarello (2003) outlined a long list of potential sources of third-party information, including personal contacts (e.g., family members, neighbors, coworkers); professional contacts (e.g., medical or

BEWARE
Be alert to the possibility of bias from third-party sources, particularly individuals with close ties to the claimant, including professional and personal contacts.

mental health professionals); personal documents (e.g., letters, journals); and professional documentation (e.g., finan-cial records, employment records, or medical records). Lewis, Rubin and Drake (2006) offered additional sugges-

BEWARE Information obtained on the Internet is not always accurate and must be verified.

tions of examining information available on the Internet, including public records, media reports, property records, and civil litigation data. They wisely caution, however, that information found on the Internet is not always accurate, and that it is important to seek verification of this data through cross-referencing multiple sources. When incorporating third-party data in an evaluation, all sources utilized by the evaluator should be explicitly identified in the writ-ten report, and information cited should always be attributed to the source (Lewis et al., 2006).

Dissimulation in Disability Claims

Estimates of the base rate of *dissimulation* in disability evaluations vary widely. Mittenberg et al. (2002) examined the rate of probable malingering and symptom exaggeration through a survey of the American Board of Clinical Neuropsychology membership. Based on a review of 3,688 disability cases, the rate of malingering or symptom exaggeration was found to be 30%. In a review of the literature, Samuel and Mittenberg (2005) reported that estimates of the base rate for malingering ranged from 7.5% to 33% of disability claimants. They suggested that malingering in disability claims can be motivated by factors such as financial incentives, socioeconomic problems, antisocial acts or behavior, career dissatisfaction, or work conflict. It appears to be well established that a certain percentage of disability claimants exaggerate, embellish, or feign their degree of impairment.

INFO Reported base rates of malingering in disability evaluations range from 7.5% to 33%.

Information regarding psychological and neuropsychological testing, including methods for detecting malingering, is avail-able to the general public. Horwitz and

McCaffrey (2006) found a number of Internet sites designed to advise individuals how to prepare for IMEs. Victor and Abeles (2004) found an Internet site with outlines of the Rorschach inkblots along with suggestions for appropriate and inappropriate responses. They also noted that a survey of trial lawyers indicated that 75% of attorneys said they spend an average of 25 to 60 minutes preparing their clients for psychological testing. Larrabee (2007) opined that, in its extreme form, coaching by attorneys can severely compromise the validity of instruments used to detect dissimulation. Thus the possibility that the claimant may be aware of and even familiar with methods for detecting exaggerated performance cannot be discounted. It should not be assumed, however, that coaching or extensive research on the part of the examinee are necessary in order to convincingly feign symptoms. Several studies have found that naïve, untrained subjects were able to successfully identify the symptoms of PTSD through uninformed guessing (Lees-Haley & Dunn, 1994; Burges & McMillan, 2001).

Sumanti et al. (2006) investigated the presence of non-credible psychiatric and cognitive symptoms in 233 "stress claim" workers' compensation litigants. They found that between 9% and 29% of the sample were identified as endorsing non-credible psychiatric symptoms using the Personality Assessment Inventory validity indices. Between 8% and 15% of the sample were documented as displaying non-credible cognitive symptomatology on the Dot Counting Test and the Rey 15-Item Test. Their data also suggested that the occurrence of psychiatric malingering was independent of feigned cognitive symptoms. This supports the notion that multiple detection strategies may be more useful than a single strategy.

BEWARE
Be aware of the possibility that the claimant may have foreknowledge of symptom validity tests obtained through research or by coaching, which could compromise the validity of these instruments.

Rogers and Payne (2006) noted that dissimulation in compensation cases extends beyond malingering *per se* to other fraudulent efforts, such as the false imputation of symptoms and impairment to compensable causes, or false claims that genuine symptoms result in diminished capacities. They noted the importance of minimizing false positives, as once a determination of malingering has been reached, this conclusion may override all other considerations and play a decisive role in the legal outcome. They recommended a multi-strategy, multi-method approach, utilizing, for example, a multiscale inventory such as the MMPI-2 and a structured interview such as the SIRS.

As noted by Farkas et al. (2006), there is no single test of malingering that acts as the "gold standard" in the detection of symptom distortion, and no single method of detecting malingering or exaggeration will be best under all circumstances (Kane, 2008). Psychometric methods available for assessing dissimulation include validity scales within tests, such as those found in the MMPI-2 and the PAI; structured interviews and self-report inventories designed to detect non-credible claims (e.g., SIRS, Miller Forensic Assessment of Symptoms Test [M-FAST], Structured Inventory of Malingered Symptomatology [SIMS]); analysis of performance patterns within tests and test batteries and correlation of real-world activities with test performance; and stand-alone tests of malingering designed to assess effort rather than impairment (e.g., Word Memory Test [WMT], VIP, Portland Digit Recognition Test [PDRT]).

Various MMPI-2 validity scales have been identified as being useful in the detection of exaggerated symptomatology. In addition to the more familiar F (infrequency) scale, support has been found for the use of the Fake Bad Scale (FBS) (Larrabee, 2002; Nelson et al., 2006; Nelson et al., 2007); the Infrequency Psychopathology scale (F_p) (Bagby et al., 2002; Elhai et al., 2004; Arbisi et al., 2006); and the Response Bias Scale (RBS) (Gervais et al., 2007; Nelson et al., 2007). Each of these scales was developed using a different methodology and for a different specific purpose. The FBS was developed by Lees-Haley et al. (1991) for use with personal injury cases, in order to detect non-credible symptom presentations as expressed in litigation settings. The Infrequency-Psychopathology scale (F_p was developed using items infrequently endorsed by psychiatric inpatients to provide a more accurate index of symptom over-reporting (Arbisi & Ben-Porath, 1995). The RBS was developed by Gervais (2005) by identifying

MMPI-2 items that were differentially endorsed by individuals passing or failing a measure of cognitive effort, the Word Memory Test.

Larrabee (2002) evaluated the usefulness of the FBS, F_p, F, and Fb validity scales of the MMPI-2 in detecting malingering neurocognitive symptoms in 33 personal injury litigants who had failed forced-choice symptom-validity testing and other measures of effort. Larrabee found the FBS was more sensitive to symptom exaggeration than F, Fb, and F_p The suspected malingerers also produced mean elevations on MMPI-2 scales 1, 3, and 7 that were significantly higher than those produced by various clinical groups, including non-litigating severe closed-head injury, multiple sclerosis, spinal cord injury, chronic pain, and depression, suggesting that MMPI-2 profiles characteristic of malingered injury differ from those associated with malingered psychopathology.

Nelson, Sweet, and Demakis (2006) investigated the usefulness of the MMPI-2 FBS scale in forensic practice through a meta-analysis of 19 studies. Their findings suggested that the FBS performed as well as, if not better than, other validity scales in discriminating over-reporting and comparison groups. They concluded that the preponderance of the present literature supported the use of the FBS within forensic settings.

Arbisi, Ben-Porath, and McNulty (2006) compared the MMPI-2 scores of compensation-seeking veterans instructed to exaggerate PTSD to those of compensation-seeking veterans instructed to respond honestly. They found the MMPI-2 F family of scales was able to accurately identify the veterans instructed to exaggerate PTSD. The F_p scale obtained the best overall hit rate in comparison to the other over-reporting indicators on the MMPI-2. The Fake Bad Scale (FBS) did not add incrementally to the prediction of exaggerated PTSD.

Gervais et al. (2008) found that elevated scores on the RBS were associated with over-reporting of memory problems, which supported the use of the RBS to detect cognitive response bias. Nelson, Sweet, and Heilbronner (2007) examined relationships of the RBS with numerous MMPI-2 validity scales in a sample of 211 participants with secondary gain or no secondary gain. They found the RBS yielded the largest effect size difference between groups, followed closely by FBS, and the L-scale. The findings suggested that RBS and FBS may represent a similar construct of symptom validity, and may outperform other MMPI-2 validity scales in discriminating between secondary gain and non-secondary gain groups.

Specialized methods for the detection of feigned psychopathology include the SIRS, the M-FAST, and the SIMS. Alwes et al. (2008) compared the effectiveness of the SIMS and the M-FAST at screening for feigned psychiatric and neurocognitive symptoms in 308 individuals undergoing neuropsychiatric evaluation for worker's compensation or personal injury claims. Examinees were assigned to probable feigning or honest groups based on results from well-validated, independent procedures. Both tests showed statistically significant discrimination between probable feigning and honest groups. Additionally, both the M-FAST and SIMS had high sensitivity and negative predictive power when discriminating between probable psychiatric feigning versus honest groups, but neither of the procedures was as effective when applied to probable neurocognitive feigners versus honest groups. These results support the use of the M-FAST and SIMS in screening for feigned psychopathology, but not for feigned neurocognitive symptoms.

In terms of stand-alone measures of symptom validity, Lynch (2004) reviewed the literature regarding the determination of effort level in forensic neurocognitive assessment. Lynch concluded that there were several effort-level measures that withstood the scrutiny of cross-validation research. These included the Computerized Assessment of Response Bias (CARB), PDRT, TOMM, VIP, Victoria Symptom Validity Test (VSVT), and WMT.

INFO

Specialized methods of detecting feigned psychopathology include structured interviews and paper and pencil tests.

Moore and Donders (2004) found that the TOMM and the California Verbal Learning Test-Second Edition (CVLT-II) were useful in assessing invalid test performance in patients with traumatic brain injuries. They studied 132 individuals who (1) had a diagnosis of TBI, defined as "an external force to the head with associated loss of consciousness," (2) were between 18 and 80 years old at the time of psychometric assessment, (3) had an absence of prior neurological or special education history, and (4) had psychometric assessment with the CVLT-II and the TOMM within one year after TBI. The results indicated that 15% of the patients performed in the invalid range. Financial compensation–seeking and psychiatric history both resulted in an almost fourfold increase in the likelihood of invalid performance on the TOMM or CVLT-II.

Rosen and Powell (2003), using a case-study approach, found that forced-choice symptom validity tests such as the Portland Digit Recognition Test could be utilized to detect malingering in claims of post-traumatic stress disorder in addition to claims of memory deficits due to brain injury.

Flaro, Green, and Robertson (2007) compared performance on the WMT of adults with TBI, tested as part of a worker's compensation, disability, or personal injury claim, with the performance of parents ordered by the court to undergo a parenting assessment. Only 60% of those in the first group, who stood to gain financially by appearing impaired on testing, performed credibly on the WMT, while 98% of those in the second group, who were motivated to do their best on testing in order to regain custody of their children, did so.

Farkas et al. (2006) attempted to systematically investigate the assumption that combining results from separate measures to detect malingering can reduce classification errors by providing convergent evidence of symptom exaggeration. They examined data from 66 disability and civil litigation evaluations to assess the degree of overlap and consistency of classification among several commonly used malingering instruments. These included validity scales from the MMPI-2 (F, F-K, F_p) and the MCMI-III (X, Z), the Rey 15-Item Test, the TOMM, and the verbal and nonverbal subtests of the VIP. Their analyses demonstrated a high degree of concordance (i.e., high correlations) among the raw scores of these multiple measures of malingering, as well as some significant discrepancies, suggesting that these scales do not overlap to the degree that the correlations might suggest. Thus, certain measures may more accurately detect certain types of distorted performance in a given set of circumstances or with certain types of claimants.

Support for aggregating results of multiple measures for the detection of dissimulation was demonstrated in a study by Larrabee (2008). The performance of litigants with definite malingering was contrasted with that of non-malingering patients with moderate and severe traumatic brain injury on five procedures: the Visual Form Discrimination Test, the Finger Tapping Test, Reliable Digit Span, Wisconsin Card Sorting Test Failure to Maintain Set score, and the FBS of the MMPI-2. The data suggested that SVT failures provided strong evidence for diagnosis of probable malingering when two SVTs were failed, and very strong evidence for probable malingering, if not definite malingering, when three SVTs were failed.

Conclusion

Although most individuals with mental health disorders are able to work, emotional and cognitive impairments can interfere significantly with their vocational performance. Individuals who receive prompt and appropriate treatment tend to have better outcomes.

Depression can affect work capacity due to physical fatigue, mildly impaired executive functions, decreased work output, impaired working memory, and impaired verbal fluency. Bipolar disorder often has an even greater effect on work functioning than does depression. Problems related to mood cycling, impaired decision making, interpersonal conflicts, impaired verbal memory, and impaired executive functions have been reported.

Anxiety disorders affect work capacity in different ways. Individuals with panic disorder, for example, tend to miss work due to avoidance behavior. Deficits in selective attention have been found in individuals with OCD. Impaired verbal memory and preoccupation with trauma may affect work capacity for those with PTSD. Alcohol abuse or dependence may have a profound impact on work performance due to time missed from work, inappropriate behavior while at work, and frontal lobe deficits. Individuals with mild cognitive disorders may have difficulty at work due to impairments in executive functions and memory.

There is no single "gold standard" for evaluating disability. Evaluations typically incorporate psychological and neuropsychological testing, self-reported information from the claimant, and third-party data. Test selection should be made on a case-by-case basis, with consideration given to the psychometric properties of the test and the legal standards for admissibility. Surveys of psychologists performing similar evaluations indicate that most evaluations include four to five tests, with the MMPI-2 being the most widely used measure. Self-report data from examinees should be evaluated in light of research that suggests that there is a tendency in circumstances where financial compensation is at stake for claimants to report better premorbid functioning and poorer current functioning than may be actually experienced.

Estimates of the base rate of malingering in disability evaluations range from 7.5% to 33%. All evaluations should incorporate an assessment of response style. The use of a multistrategy, multimethod approach is recommended, utilizing a combination of psychometric approaches such as multiscale inventories, structured interviews, and stand-alone symptom validity tests. Data from these instruments should be incorporated with data obtained from third-party sources in order to obtain a more complete and accurate understanding of the claimant's condition and functioning.

APPLICATION

A disability evaluation requires significant preparation, beginning well before the claimant walks into the evaluator's office. Such preparation will help the evaluator avoid referrals that may be inappropriate, ensure that relevant and sufficient data are efficiently collected during the evaluation, and facilitate compliance with ethical and legal requirements.

Initial Contacts

The disability evaluation process is initiated when the potential evaluator is contacted by the referral source. Referrals generally come from one of three sources. The evaluator may be contacted directly by the insurance company or agency responsible for providing the disability benefits, by an attorney representing the claimant or the insurance company, or by an independent vendor. The first contact usually is an inquiry about the evaluator's availability, the expected time frame, and a general sense of the key issues to be addressed in the evaluation.

Typically, the evaluator is also provided with the name of the claimant as well as his or her treatment providers and (if represented) attorney to determine if there is any conflict of interest that would keep the evaluator from accepting the referral. The evaluator's fees and cancellation policy are usually discussed as well. Although these questions may appear to be perfunctory, they are actually very

INFO

Referrals for disability evaluations may come from the disability insurance company, an attorney representing the claimant or the company, or an independent vendor.

important—and should be carefully considered before agreeing to accept the referral. As noted in the Specialty Guidelines for Forensic Psychologists:

> During initial consultation with the legal representative of the party seeking services, forensic psychologists have an obligation to inform the party of factors that might reasonably affect the decision to contract with the forensic psychologist. These factors include, but are not limited to, the fee structure for anticipated professional services; prior and current personal or professional activities, obligations, and relationships that might produce a conflict of interests; their areas of competence and the limits of their competence; and the known scientific bases and limitations of the methods and procedures that they employ and their qualifications to employ such methods and procedures (Committee on Ethical Guidelines for Forensic Psychologists, 1991, p. 658).

Practical Concerns

Disability evaluations are complex and time-consuming. As will be discussed in detail in the next chapter, a typical disability evaluation consists of a thorough clinical interview, the administration of a battery of psychological and/or neuropsychological tests, a review of written records (which are often quite substantial), interviews with collateral sources, and a detailed and comprehensive written report. The evaluator must be confident that he or she can accomplish this within a reasonable time period without compromising the quality of the evaluation. Insurance companies typically expect to receive the evaluator's report within two weeks of the completion of the evaluation.

Consideration should also be given to any logistical issues presented by the referral. Does the claimant require special accommodations for

BEST PRACTICE

Before accepting a referral, be sure to consider the following:

- Conflict of interest/multiple relationship
- Time constraints/scheduling availability
- Competence/expertise
- Access to necessary psychometric instruments
- Financial arrangements

mobility, such as an elevator or ramp? Will the claimant be examined at the evaluator's office, or will the evaluator need to travel to an offsite location to perform the evaluation? If travel is required, how will arrangements be made? How can the evaluator ensure that sufficient time is allowed to complete the evaluation?

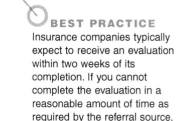

BEST PRACTICE
Insurance companies typically expect to receive an evaluation within two weeks of its completion. If you cannot complete the evaluation in a reasonable amount of time as required by the referral source, do not accept the referral.

Will a suitable venue—one that is sufficiently quiet, private, well lighted, and appropriately furnished—be available for the evaluation? Will the evaluator have difficulty transporting testing materials and necessary equipment to an offsite location?

The evaluator should be prepared to clarify the financial arrangements for the evaluation in the first contact with the referral source. As stated in the American Psychological Association (APA) Code of Ethics (2002) (Section 6.04): "As early as is feasible in a professional or scientific relationship, psychologists and recipients of psychological services reach an agreement specifying compensation and billing arrangements"; and in Section 6.06: "In their reports to payors for services . . ., psychologists take reasonable steps to ensure the accurate reporting of the nature of the service provided . . ., the fees, charges, or payments, and where applicable, the identity of the provider, the findings, and the diagnosis."

4
chapter

In a disability evaluation, the fee should be defined either as an hourly rate or as a flat fee. In the case of the former, the evaluator should plan to present an itemized invoice at the conclusion of the evaluation, with a clear accounting of the billed hours. The use of a flat fee is not recommended, as it presents numerous problems and risks to the evaluator, especially if he or she discovers that the amount of work required to evaluate the claimant has been significantly underestimated. This places the evaluator in the uncomfortable position of having to do work without compensation or perform a less-comprehensive evaluation than is

BEST PRACTICE
Clarify all financial arrangements with the referral source prior to beginning the evaluation.

BEWARE
Never
agree to financial compensation
contingent upon the outcome
of a case.

required (which would be inappropriate). If the evaluator chooses to bill the evaluation as a flat fee, there should be no adjustments or changes in the final bill unless the evaluator is specifically asked and agrees to expand the scope of the evaluation in some substantial way. If the evaluator foresees any additional charges (e.g., fees for testing materials, travel expenses), such fees should be disclosed in the initial contact with the referral source. The evaluator should also outline his or her policy with regard to a cancellation or "no-show" fee. For example, the evaluator might decide to charge a fee equivalent to two to four hours time if the evaluation is cancelled with less than forty-eight hours' notice. The amount to be charged and the time frame for notice of cancellation should be clearly communicated to the referral source.

Competence and Expertise

The next consideration before accepting a referral is whether the evaluator has the requisite expertise to perform the evaluation being requested. Both the APA Ethics Code and the Specialty Guidelines for Forensic Psychologists explicitly address the importance of practicing within the limits of one's competence. The APA Ethics Code (2002) states in Section 2.01 (a): "Psychologists provide services . . . with populations and in areas only within the boundaries of their competence, based on their education, training, supervised experience, consultation, study, or professional experience." The Specialty Guidelines note: "Forensic psychologists provide services only in areas of psychology in which they have specialized knowledge, skill, experience, and education" (1991, p. 658).

Factors related to the issues presented by the referral and the claimant's characteristics should be considered in assessing competence. Section 2.01 (b) of the APA Ethics Code addresses this as well:

BEWARE
Never
accept referrals that are outside
the limits of your competence.

Where scientific or professional knowledge in the discipline of psychology establishes that an understanding of factors associated with age, gender, gender identity, race, ethnicity, culture, national origin, religion, sexual orientation, disability, language, or socioeconomic status is essential for effective implementation of their services or research, psychologists have or obtain the training, experience, consultation, or supervision necessary to ensure the competence of their services, or they make appropriate referrals. . . .

At times the evaluator may be unsure whether to accept or decline a referral. Before accepting a referral, the evaluator should consider if he or she has sufficient experience with the diagnosis presented by the claimant. This is especially important when the claimant presents with an unusual diagnosis that requires specialized knowledge (e.g., gender identity disorder, fentanyl addiction, toxic exposure) or characteristics related to ethnic or cultural factors, language fluency, or age with which the evaluator is not sufficiently familiar. The evaluator should also consider the assessment methods and tools that might be required to perform the evaluation. The evaluator should be proficient in the use of, and have readily available, all assessment instruments necessary to address the referral questions.

Conflicts of Interest and Multiple Relationships

Conflicts of interest can compromise the objectivity and integrity of a forensic evaluation. As defined in the APA Ethics Code, Section 3.06:

Psychologists refrain from taking on a professional role when personal, scientific, professional, legal, financial, or other interests or relationships could reasonably be expected to (1) impair their objectivity, competence, or effectiveness in performing their functions as psychologists, or (2) expose the person or

BEST PRACTICE
Ensure that you have the proper qualifications for the referral case, including the required

- Knowledge
- Training
- Skill set
- Experience

organization with whom the professional relationship exists to harm or exploitation (2002).

Similarly, multiple relationships can impair an evaluator's objectivity and effectiveness:

> A multiple relationship occurs when a psychologist is in a professional role with a person and (1) at the same time is in another role with the same person, (2) at the same time is in a relationship with a person closely associated with or related to the person with whom the psychologist has the professional relationship, or (3) promises to enter into another relationship in the future with the person or a person closely associated with or related to the person (APA, 2002, Section 3.05).

The Specialty Guidelines for Forensic Psychologists also address this issue:

> Forensic psychologists recognize potential conflicts of interest in dual relationships with parties to a legal proceeding, and they seek to minimize their effects. Forensic psychologists avoid providing professional services to parties in a legal proceeding with whom they have personal or professional relationships that are inconsistent with the anticipated relationship (1991, p. 659).

The following examples would probably constitute a significant conflict of interest. An evaluator should avoid accepting a referral for a disability evaluation in any of the following circumstances:

- The claimant or any member of his or her immediate family is or has been treated by the evaluator. (Example: the evaluator is treating the claimant's brother.)

- The claimant or any member of his or her immediate family has or has had a personal, social, business, or professional relationship with the evaluator or any member of the evaluator's immediate family. (Example: the claimant's wife is the teacher of the evaluator's daughter.)

- The evaluator has a close and ongoing personal, social, business, or professional relationship with the claimant's treatment providers or attorney. (Example: the claimant's attorney is representing the evaluator in a civil lawsuit.)

This list is far from exhaustive. The evaluator should carefully consider any circumstance that presents (or would appear to present) any threat to the impartiality of the evaluation.

One type of multiple relationship that has received considerable attention is the role-conflict inherent in providing both treatment and forensic evaluation to the same individual. Engaging in the dual role of therapist-evaluator threatens the objectivity and integrity of the evaluation. As noted by Kane (2008), the roles of therapist and forensic evaluator are significantly different and nearly always conflict with each other. Greenberg and Shuman (1997) enumerate ten key differences between therapeutic and forensic roles that illustrate how combining these roles compromises both the efficacy of therapy and the objectivity of the forensic evaluation. Likewise, Strasberger, Gutheil, and Brodsky (1997) note that attempting to treat and evaluate the same person creates an irreconcilable role-conflict that manifests itself in different conceptions of truth and causation, different forms of alliance, different types of assessment, and different ethical guidelines.

The potential evaluator should immediately disclose to the referral source any foreseeable conflicts of interest, multiple relationships, or the existence of any circumstance that might appear to an outside observer to be a conflict of interest. Even if the association is limited or insignificant and the evaluator feels certain that his or her objectivity would not be compromised, the referral source should be given the opportunity to make an informed decision about how to proceed.

Defining the Scope of the Evaluation

Once the evaluator has accepted the referral, the focus shifts to delineating

BEWARE Conflicts of interest and multiple relationships can impair objectivity and the integrity of the evaluation. Do not accept evaluation referrals when these factors are present.

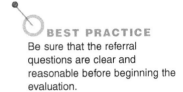

the psycho-legal questions to be addressed in the evaluation and the formulation of detailed plans to answer these questions. The referral source should have provided a list of "referral questions" to be addressed in the evaluation. If not, the evaluator should contact the referral source and request clarification. The evaluator needs to ascertain if the questions being asked can be reasonably addressed in an evaluation, and if sufficient data will be available to formulate an opinion.

It is not uncommon for referral questions to be couched in terms in terms that cannot be answered directly with psychological or neuropsychological evaluation. As described in detail in Chapter 2, it is up to the evaluator to determine how the questions relate to psychological and cognitive functional capacities that can be assessed in the evaluation. Referral questions will often ask the evaluator to (a) describe the symptoms of the claimant's alleged condition, (b) determine if these symptoms support a particular diagnosis or diagnoses, (c) comment on the credibility of the claimant's presentation, and (d) describe how the symptoms affect the claimant's work capacity. Other questions may relate to the nature and appropriateness of the claimant's treatment, and the prognosis and estimated time for functional recovery.

The evaluator must remain focused on the critical issues to be addressed in the evaluation, so that relevant data can be obtained. For example, is this a new claim of disability in which the presence of a condition has yet to be established? Or has the claimant been receiving benefits for some time, and there are now questions about the extent of the claimant's progress and recovery? Is the claimant's ability to perform the duties of his or her own occupation at issue, or is the ability to work in any occupation relevant? Are the concerns solely with the claimant's ability to return to work on a full-time basis, or should his or her ability to work part-time be considered? Have there been prior evaluations of this claimant that have yielded conflicting results requiring some type of resolution?

Occasionally, referral questions will ask for a direct opinion on the ultimate issue: is the claimant entitled to receive disability benefits? As discussed elsewhere in this volume, this is not a question that can be meaningfully answered by the evaluator. Eligibility for benefits is determined by an analysis of the functional capacity of the claimant in combination with a number of other factors, including the specific provisions of the policy, information regarding the claimant's occupational activities, and other factors that might affect the claimant's eligibility to receive benefits. Consequently, the evaluator should not provide an opinion on the ultimate issue. The evaluator should consider how factors obtainable in the evaluation could assist the insurance company personnel in reaching a sound decision, and focus on providing these data.

The evaluator then must define the specific scope and nature of the evaluation. Disability evaluations typically include multiple sources of data (e.g., testing, self-report, collateral, and written records). The evaluator should review the referral questions and the written data provided by the referral source in order to determine if sufficient data have been provided, what additional data will be needed, which psychological tests will be used, and which collateral sources might be available to provide relevant information. If the material provided is incomplete, the evaluator should contact the referral source immediately to address this situation.

Sometimes the information provided by the insurance company may contain terms and concepts specific to the insurance industry that are unfamiliar to the evaluator (see Table 4.1). Vore (2007) noted, "The language used in the disability insurance industry is specific to contractual issues related to the policies issued by the carriers. . . . [Without clear] understanding, the opinion presented in the report regarding the evaluation completed may be irrelevant to the issues at hand, and, therefore of limited or no use to the carrier in the claims management process." It is important to clarify any areas of

BEWARE
It is not your role as an evaluator to determine the ultimate legal issue. Do not provide your opinion as to whether or not the claimant is entitled to receive disability benefits. Instead, focus your opinion on the claimant's work capacity.

Table 4.1 | Disability Insurance Terms and Concepts

- **Total Disability**—the claimant is unable to carry out any or all of his/her important occupational duties.

- **Partial Disability**—the claimant is unable to carry out some or most of his/her important occupational duties.

- **Residual Disability**—the claimant can perform some or most of his/her important occupational duties, but cannot do so at his/her previous level of functioning resulting in a loss of income.

- **Elimination Period**—the period of time defined in the policy between the onset of the disability and the time at which benefits become payable.

- **Own Occupation**—the claimant is entitled to disability benefits if he/she is unable to perform the duties of his/her own occupation, regardless of whether or not he/she could perform some other occupation.

- **Any Occupation**—the claimant is entitled to benefits only if he/she cannot perform any occupation which is roughly commensurate in terms of educational requirements and earning potential with his/her own occupation.

confusion prior to beginning the evaluation by contacting the referral source.

The evaluator should carefully review the written records provided to ensure they are complete and sufficient, and arrange the material in chronological order to facilitate review and double-check completeness. Relevant dates, including when the claimant stopped working, filed for disability, and began treatment, should be provided. There should be a list of, and contact information for, the claimant's treatment providers. Treatment records should be legible and dated. Comprehensive information regarding the claimant's occupation, including a detailed job description, should be provided. The evaluator should assess the volume and nature of the records to determine a rough estimate of the time that should be allotted for a thorough review of this material. It is important to perform a comprehensive review of the written records prior to meeting the claimant, as this will ensure that the appropriate issues will be addressed in the evaluation. If the evaluator determines that important records are absent, incomplete or illegible, the referral source should be contacted immediately.

If psychological or neuropsychological testing will be included in the evaluation, consideration should be

given to the selection of appropriate instruments. It may be wise to develop "contingency plans" in the event that an originally selected instrument cannot be used for some reason. For example, if the evaluator discovers upon interviewing the claimant that he or she was administered the Wechsler Memory Scale two weeks before, it may be necessary to assess the claimant's memory with another measure. The evaluator should determine the sequence in which the instruments will be administered, making sure that adequate time is allotted.

In some circumstances, the evaluator may find it helpful to review recent literature related to issues in the evaluation. This is particularly important when the claimant presents with an unusual diagnosis or symptoms, or is engaged in a new form of treatment. It may also be helpful to review literature related to the claimant's cultural background as it relates to the presentation of symptoms or other aspects of behavior relevant to the evaluation. Sometimes the evaluator may need to obtain more information about the nature of the claimant's occupation in order to be prepared for the evaluation.

4
chapter

Contact with Referral Sources, Attorneys, and Claimants

It is important for the evaluator to remember that the "client" is the party or entity requesting the evaluation. Questions, requests for additional materials or records, and logistical issues should all be directed to the referral source. Although many disability claimants are not represented by counsel, the evaluator may occasionally be contacted by an attorney representing the claimant. Attorneys may request information about the content of the proposed evaluation or the qualifications of the evaluator. They may also attempt

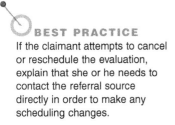

to cancel or reschedule the evaluation, demand to be present during the evaluation, ask to have the evaluation video- or audio-recorded, or request a copy of the report or the raw data. If contacted by an attorney by telephone or in writing, the evaluator should consult with the referral source rather than responding directly to the attorney. The evaluator should be prepared to discuss his or her views on these matters with the referral source, if such requests threaten the integrity or validity of the evaluation.

Prior to beginning the evaluation, the evaluator typically has little or no direct contact with the claimant. Thus scheduling problems, logistical issues, and other arrangements should be addressed through the referral source rather than directly with the claimant. If the claimant contacts the evaluator to cancel or reschedule the evaluation or to request a change to the format or structure of the evaluation, the evaluator should explain to the claimant that that the nature of the evaluation is in response to the company's request, and the claimant needs to deal directly with the company regarding the evaluation and its scheduling. The evaluator should also communicate this information to the referral source.

Logistics and Schedules

The evaluator's next task is to determine when and how the evaluation will be conducted. The referral source, in consultation with the claimant, may make specific requests in this regard. For example, some claimants may want to break up the evaluation into several shorter sessions rather than one long session. Others may be traveling from some distance away and are not able to return for multiple sessions. Some claimants may object to arriving early in the morning or staying later in the day. Other claimants may have concerns regarding transportation to the evaluator's office.

Some claimants request specific accommodations such as ergonomic chairs or special lighting. At times, a claimant may be unwilling or unable to travel to the evaluator's office, requiring the evaluator to travel to a location nearer the claimant. When faced with special requests, the evaluator should consider the extent to which these requests can be reasonably accommodated without compromising the integrity or validity of the evaluation, while balancing the claimant's needs and the evaluator's availability. For example, breaking an eight-hour evaluation into two four-hour sessions is usually not a problem. On the other hand, breaking it into sixteen half-hour sessions might not be feasible.

There may be occasions in which the claimant fails to appear for the scheduled evaluation or arrives much later than anticipated. When a claimant fails to arrive within thirty minutes of the scheduled time, the evaluator should notify the referral source. The referral source will attempt to contact the claimant and resolve the situation. When a claimant arrives an hour or more late for the evaluation, the evaluator must decide if completing the evaluation on the same day is possible. If not, the referral source should be notified so that other scheduling arrangements can be made.

Occasionally the evaluator will become aware of previously unknown circumstances that suggest that his or her initial estimate of the time involved in performing the evaluation was insufficient. This may be due to the volume of written records, the nature of the claimant's difficulties, or scheduling issues on the part of the claimant. When the evaluator determines that the actual amount of time needed to complete the evaluation is substantially different than what was agreed upon with the referral source, the evaluator should immediately consult with the referral source before proceeding. In most cases, the referral source will authorize the additional time if the request is reasonable. The important thing is to communicate clearly with the referral source about any significant changes in circumstances.

When the evaluator is asked to travel to the claimant to perform an

BEST PRACTICE
Always communicate with the referral source about any significant changes in circumstances that may substantially change the amount of time needed to conduct the evaluation.

evaluation, additional considerations arise. There should be a discussion with the referral source and a clear understanding developed of how the evaluator will be compensated for his or her travel time and expenses. This is especially important when overnight travel is required. If the evaluator is required to travel to a different state or province, she or he should determine if professional licensing will be an issue. It is advisable to contact the local state or provincial licensing board when contemplating performing an evaluation in a jurisdiction in which the evaluator is not licensed to determine what, if any, arrangements must be made. The evaluator needs to ensure that an appropriate site for the evaluation, such as a hotel conference room, is arranged. There must be adequate lighting, an appropriate work surface, privacy, and quiet. The evaluator must arrange to transport all the materials needed for the evaluation. This requires advance consideration of which psychological tests will be used, including alternate choices if some problem arises that prevents the evaluator from using the original instruments.

Occasionally the claimant, without prior notice, may arrive for the evaluation with an attorney, family member, or other party with the expectation that this person will sit in on the evaluation as an observer, or bring an audio- or video-recording device. To avoid being blindsided by such requests, the evaluator should give consideration to this issue prior to beginning the evaluation process. It is important for the evaluator to be able to cogently explain the reasoning behind his or her position on these issues. When such requests are made without advance notice, the evaluator should consult with the referral source immediately and be prepared to discuss how the presence of an observer or recording device might affect the evaluation, and the circumstances under which this would and would not be acceptable to the evaluator.

Authorization and Consent

The Referral Source

Given that the referral source is the evaluator's "client," the evaluator must confer with the referral source before releasing any information or making any decisions to change the nature, structure, content, or scope of the evaluation. The disability evaluator must remain aware of the context of the evaluation—specifically, whether the evaluation is occurring during the claim adjudication process or during litigation. Among the reasons for attending to this distinction is the fact that information given to the evaluator by the referral source is confidential during the claims adjudication process. Thus, the evaluator has no authority to share information provided by the referral source with any other party, including the claimant, the claimant's attorney, or any collateral contact. This includes information regarding the adjudication process of the claim, the existence or content of medical records, claim forms, and investigative reports.

Likewise, the evaluator should refrain from expanding or changing the agreed-upon scope of the evaluation. For example, if the evaluator has been asked to perform a neuropsychological evaluation related to a head injury, the evaluator should not unilaterally decide to expand the scope of the evaluation to include an assessment of psychopathology without consulting with the referral source. Decisions regarding whether (and by whom) the evaluation may be recorded, or if an observer is allowed to sit in, should also be made in consultation with the referral source. In addition, the evaluator does not have the authority to release any information about the findings, content, or outcome of the evaluation to any party other than the referral source without prior authorization. This includes providing feedback, either verbally or in written form, to the claimant, the claimant's attorney, or the claimant's treatment provider, including offering suggestions about improving or changing the claimant's treatment.

The Claimant

As the individual being evaluated, the claimant must consent to the evaluation before any aspect of the evaluation begins. The evaluator cannot compel the claimant to participate in the evaluation. If the claimant refuses to consent, the evaluator should immediately cease the evaluation and communicate this information to the referral source.

INFO

Elements of informed consent for disability evaluation:

- Identification of referring party
- Reason for evaluation
- Identification of evaluator
- Role of evaluator
- Description of evaluation
- Confidentiality limits
- Access to evaluation data
- Participation is voluntary
- No treatment offered

Obtaining informed consent from the examinee is mandated by professional ethics. The APA Ethics Code (Section 3.10) states, "When psychologists conduct research or provide assessment, therapy, counseling, or consulting services in person or via electronic transmission or other forms of communication, they obtain the informed consent of the individual or individuals using language that is reasonably understandable to that person or persons. . . . Psychologists appropriately document written or oral consent, permission, and assent." Also in Section 4.02:

Psychologists discuss with persons (including, to the extent feasible, persons who are legally incapable of giving informed consent and their legal representatives) and organizations with whom they establish a scientific or professional relationship (1) the relevant limits of confidentiality and (2) the foreseeable uses of the information generated through their psychological activities. . . . Unless it is not feasible or is contraindicated, the discussion of confidentiality occurs at the outset of the relationship and thereafter as new circumstances may warrant.

The Specialty Guidelines for Forensic Psychology state,

Forensic psychologists have an obligation to ensure that prospective clients are informed of their legal rights with respect to the anticipated forensic service, of the purposes of any evaluation, of the nature of procedures to be employed, of the intended uses of any product of their services, and of the party who has employed the forensic psychologist. . . . Forensic psychologists inform their clients of the limitations to the confidentiality of their services and their products by providing them with an understandable statement of their rights, privileges, and the limitations of confidentiality (1991, p. 659).

In a disability evaluation, the claimant should be given a detailed explanation of the evaluation and its purpose, identification of the evaluator's role, information regarding the individual or entity requesting the evaluation, an explanation of the limits of confidentiality, and the fact that the evaluator cannot release information regarding the findings of the evaluation to the claimant. It should be clearly stated that the claimant is not being offered treatment. This information should be provided both verbally and in writing. Prior to signing the consent form, the claimant should be asked to paraphrase her or his understanding of the information and should be given ample opportunity to ask questions about the evaluation. If the claimant voices concerns or does not appear to understand significant aspects of the evaluation process, the referral source should be consulted and a plan should be developed to respond to the claimant's concerns. A claimant who is represented by counsel may wish to contact his or her attorney before proceeding.

In addition to consenting to participate in the evaluation, authorization from the claimant must be sought before the evaluator can contact collateral sources. The evaluator may address this at the outset of the evaluation or at some other point in the evaluation process. Written authorizations, consistent with federal and local standards, should be utilized. As noted in the Specialty Guidelines for Forensic Psychologists (1991, p. 662), "When forensic psychologists seek data from third parties, prior records, or other sources, they do so only with the prior approval of the relevant legal party or as a consequence of an order of a court to conduct the forensic evaluation."

4
chapter

Collateral Sources

Although the claimant must grant permission for the evaluator to contact collateral sources, it is not necessary to obtain a signed authorization or consent

BEWARE
Never contact collateral sources without first obtaining written authorization from the claimant.

from the actual source. When contacting a collateral source by telephone, the evaluator should clearly state the reason for the consultation, the evaluator's role, and the intended use of the data, including the fact that the information obtained will be attributed to the source. The evaluator should obtain the informed "assent" of the collateral source before any discussion begins. Medical doctors, particularly primary-care physicians, are often contacted by mental health professionals who are treating their patients in order to coordinate treatment. It is important to make it clear that this is not the reason for the evaluator's call; the evaluator's role is of a forensic evaluator, and not a treatment provider.

Collateral sources often include people whose relationship with the claimant is not a professional one. Family members, neighbors, business associates, and others may be appropriate collateral contacts in a given evaluation. Such individuals are not usually in the habit of sharing information about other people with mental health professionals. They may be unfamiliar with the context of a disability evaluation. Thus it is particularly important when contacting nonprofessional collateral sources, whether by telephone or in a face-to-face interview, to carefully explain the reason for the interview and how the information will be used.

Sometimes a claimant will refuse to allow the evaluator to contact collateral sources. If so, the evaluator should explain to the claimant the importance of this and attempt to determine the nature of the claimant's concerns. Such concerns typically fall into one of several categories: (1) the claimant views the evaluator as an agent of the insurance company and is reluctant to allow the evaluator access to additional personal information—this usually arises when the evaluator wants to speak to the claimant's psychotherapist or a family member; (2) the claimant fears the evaluator will disclose information to the collateral source that she or he wishes to keep private—this usually occurs when the collateral source is a business or professional contact; (3) the claimant suspects that the collateral source will communicate information that is unfavorable to his or her claim for disability benefits; and (4) the claimant's attorney has instructed her or him not to authorize such contact. In general, claimants may be more willing to provide the evaluator with permission to contact collateral sources at the conclusion of the evaluation, when the evaluator has presumably demonstrated his or her commitment to be fair and objective. If, however, the claimant continues to refuse access to collateral sources, the evaluator should document this in the report and note any limitations resulting from this.

Documentation

Creating and maintaining appropriate written and/or electronic documentation of the evaluation is critical. The evaluator should develop a system for effectively documenting all aspects of the evaluation beginning with the first contact by the referral source. Indeed, the importance of documentation in the forensic context is even higher than it is for treatment (Committee for Specialty Guidelines for Forensic Psychologists, 1991).

Many evaluators develop forms or other paperwork to facilitate the collection of factual information, record the claimant's contact and identifying information, and document the time spent on various aspects of the evaluation. As previously discussed in detail, written documentation of informed consent and authorization to contact collateral sources is strongly recommended and may be required by some referral sources. All data, including notes from interviews with the claimant and with collateral sources, raw

test data, and other written material documenting any aspect of the evaluation, must be preserved and maintained as part of the evaluator's file. The Specialty Guidelines for Forensic Psychologists support this as well, noting that forensic psychologists have an obligation to document all data that form the basis for their evidence or services.

As noted earlier in this chapter, the evaluator is often provided with a large volume of written records or other materials from the referral source, such as surveillance videos, to review. It is important for the evaluator to retain as a part of his or her file the documentation that formed the foundation of the evaluator's opinion. At times, the evaluator may be asked to return such data to the referral source at the completion of the evaluation. If possible, the evaluator should try to explain to the referral source why it would be important for the evaluator to retain this information. While it is acceptable to return copies of material provided by the referral source, under no circumstances should the evaluator relinquish the only copies of original material produced during the course of the evaluation. If such information is requested by the referral source, the evaluator should provide copies and retain the originals in his or her file.

Adjudication versus Litigation

Most requests for disability evaluations originate during the course of the adjudication of the claim rather than during litigation. Most claim disputes do not go on to litigation. However, the evaluator should approach every disability evaluation by anticipating that the case could end up in litigation. By operating in this fashion, the evaluator will ensure compliance with the highest standards. This

includes choosing evaluation methodologies that will meet the relevant admissibility standards, and maintaining and preserving the data of the evaluation in anticipation of its use as evidence in a legal proceeding. The evaluator should expect that his or her report and records will be discoverable in an adversarial forum and that the evaluator's testimony will be required. The only way to ensure that the evaluator will be able to meet these demands is through systematic planning from the start of the evaluation through its completion.

Conclusion

This chapter described the need for careful planning and attention to detail prior to beginning the actual evaluation. When presented with a potential referral, the evaluator should consider several factors before accepting. These include possible conflicts of interest, required expertise, time constraints, and access to needed materials and instruments. Financial arrangements should be clarified with the referral source before beginning the evaluation. The referral questions must be translated into measurable psycho-legal constructs. The evaluator should review the material provided by the referral source for completeness and legibility. The evaluator must be aware of the context of the evaluation and how this relates to issues of confidentiality and privilege, especially in terms of the release of data both provided by the referral source and obtained in the course of the evaluation. It is necessary to obtain and document informed consent from the claimant before the evaluation can begin. In addition, when incorporating information from collateral sources, the evaluator needs to obtain both authorization from the claimant and assent from the collateral source. All the data obtained during the course of the evaluation or provided to the evaluator that form the basis of the evaluator's opinion must be preserved in the evaluator's file. The evaluator should approach all disability evaluations with the anticipation that litigation is possible, so that the evaluator's methods and data will meet admissibility standards and will allow the evaluator to effectively testify in a deposition or at trial. This careful preparation lays the groundwork for data collection, which will be addressed in Chapter 5, and interpretation of these data, which will be addressed in Chapter 6.

Data Collection | 5

This chapter will present a structure for the collection of data during the disability evaluation, emphasizing the specific methodology for obtaining data from various sources. These sources include written records and documents, self-report data from the claimant, psychological and neuropsychological test data, and information from collaterals. It is important that the evaluator collect sufficient and valid data in the course of the evaluation, as this will provide the foundation for the evaluator's opinions.

Data Sources

The use of multiple sources of data is essential for a comprehensive assessment. Thus, the first step in the IME process is to identify potential data sources and determine appropriate methods of data collection for each source. Typically, data sources include written documents and records, information obtained directly from the claimant, data from psychometric assessment, and information obtained from collateral sources. By utilizing a variety of sources, the evaluator will be able to compare information obtained from each source to obtain a more complete and objective understanding of the claimant's condition and functional capacity.

Although there are many different ways to structure the IME, data collection usually proceeds in the following sequence:

1. Prior to meeting with the claimant:
   a. Review records
   b. Formulate evaluation strategies

    c. Check to be sure all relevant material has been provided

2. Meet with the claimant:

    a. Obtain informed consent

    b. Interview the claimant

3. Administer psychological and/or neuropsychological tests and response-style measures

4. Concluding discussion with the claimant:

    a. Clarify any issues raised by testing

    b. Obtain permission to contact collateral sources

5. Interview collateral sources

Reviewing Records

Reviewing the written documents and records provided by the referral source is usually the first step in data collection and should be undertaken before the claimant is seen by the evaluator. This allows the evaluator to gain an overview of the issues in question, to determine if additional records will be needed, and to become familiar with the claimant's history and circumstances. The quality and volume of written documentation varies greatly. The evaluator should check that the documentation provided is sufficient and legible. If not, the evaluator should immediately contact the referral source to correct this situation. Records that are incomplete or unreadable cannot provide the evaluator with the information needed to complete the evaluation and may yield a misleading picture of the claimant's situation. Table 5.1 provides a list of records and documents for review.

It is important to allow sufficient time to review records. The evaluator can ask the referral source in advance about the volume of records that will be provided. When the records are received, the evaluator should organize the records chronologically and by source. It is often helpful to create an outline or

BEST PRACTICE
If the documentation you have been given is incomplete or insufficient, contact the referral source immediately.

Table 5.1 | Records and Documents for Review

Essential Records	Very Useful Records	Additional Records
Current treatment records related to cause of disability	Past treatment records related to cause of disability	Past primary care records
Claim forms describing cause of disability and date of onset	Investigative reports	Other general medical records
Job description	Financial records	Insurance company documents and memos
	Primary care records	
	Prior evaluation reports	
	In-house consultant reports	

spreadsheet summarizing the material and listing the source, dates, and contents of the records.

Once an overview of the records is completed, the evaluator can begin to review the documentation in detail. There are many different strategies that can facilitate this, depending on the type and volume of the records and the evaluator's preferences. It is generally most efficient to make notes while reviewing the records. When the volume of records is large, it may be convenient to dictate notes using a digital voice recorder or voice-recognition software. The use of document flags can help the evaluator quickly locate key material later on.

Contemporaneous documentation is very helpful in establishing an understanding of the claimant's condition and functioning over time. Not all documentation is equally useful, however. The evaluator needs to consider the database and methodology that

were used to create the documentation. If the documentation was based on incorrect or incomplete information or created using unreliable methods, the value of the documentation will be diminished. The evaluator should always seek to use primary rather than secondary sources. For example, the evaluator should not rely on a reviewer's summary of medical records, but should examine the actual records themselves.

During the course of the evaluation, the evaluator may discover the existence of additional records beyond those provided for review. For example, during the interview the claimant may disclose that he recently sought treatment from a new psychiatrist. In this event, the evaluator should contact the referral source and request that these records be obtained. The evaluator should not undertake to obtain records independently unless so directed by the referral source.

In the event that certain records cannot be obtained (or cannot be obtained within a reasonable timeframe), the evaluator must decide how to proceed. In most cases, the evaluator can continue with the report, noting any limitations resulting from the lack of specific documentation. For example, the evaluator might indicate that, although the claimant reported that she received ECT in the 1990's, the records documenting this could not be obtained. Only in the most extreme circumstances, and after discussing the situation with the referral source, should the evaluator consider not completing the evaluation or delaying the report indefinitely pending the receipt of additional records. This would apply only in situations in which the evaluator determines that the missing data are crucial to the evaluation process, and without them an accurate opinion cannot be formulated.

Treatment records, including psychotherapeutic, psychiatric, substance abuse, hospital, and medical records, can provide valuable information about the onset of the claimant's difficulties, the progression of symptoms, his efforts to seek treatment, and his response to treatment. The evaluator should note the nature and frequency of the claimant's treatment and whether it appears to be consistent with the claimant's reported condition. Particular attention should be paid to changes in treatment such as increases or decreases in treatment frequency, medications prescribed, referrals for adjunct treatment, or gaps in treatment. If the claimant has been treated by multiple providers, it is useful to compare each provider's impressions of the claimant.

Sometimes the evaluator will be provided with prior evaluations of the claimant to review. In doing so, several factors must be considered:

- Was the evaluation done by an independent provider for evaluative or forensic purposes, or was it obtained by the claimant for treatment purposes?
- Does the report provide enough data to support the opinions expressed?
- Are test scores included so that the evaluator can assess the accuracy of the interpretation?
- Was the evaluation performed by someone with appropriate credentials and adequate training?
- If the prior evaluation was done to assess disability, was the context and benefit source the same as for the present evaluation?

As described in Chapter 1, different benefit sources utilize different definitions of disability and different methods of disability determination. Social Security disability, in particular, follows a very specific set of procedures. It is important to take this into consideration when reviewing documentation related to other sources of disability benefits.

Investigative reports may be included in the records provided for review. Investigators are sometimes used by the insurance industry to document a claimant's activities. The products of these investigations typically consist of a written report (including a timeline and a description of the investigator's observations), still photographs, and video. When such material is available, it is important that the evaluator view the actual video and not simply rely on the investigator's written descriptions.

Although surveillance is often of limited use in clarifying psychiatric functioning, it may highlight inconsistencies between the claimant's reported condition and activities and what was observed by the investigator. For example, the credibility of the claimant's self-report might be questioned when she maintains that she does not get out of bed until noon because of depression, yet is observed on a surveillance video leaving the house at 6:00 A.M. to go the gym. The evaluator may also compare the claimant's appearance on the video in terms of dress, grooming, and affect with her appearance during the IME.

It is important not to overvalue the data obtained through surveillance. The evaluator should bear in mind that surveillance data are a small sampling of the claimant's behavior and may not be representative of the claimant's typical functioning. If the evaluator's opinion rests in part on surveillance data, it should be made clear that such data were only one of many factors considered in formulating the evaluator's final opinion.

Employment and financial records are useful in understanding the claimant's occupational functioning prior to the onset of the claimed disability. For example, such records can address questions regarding the claimant's earnings, the claimant's work performance, and the consistency of the claimant's work history. The evaluator should note disciplinary actions, performance evaluations, and significant changes in earnings. Financial and employment data may also help verify the claimant's report regarding his job duties and work schedule. Regardless of what other employment or financial records are provided, the one essential document that must be reviewed is a detailed job description. The evaluator will not be able to complete the IME without a clear understanding of the claimant's job duties and responsibilities.

The evaluator will probably be provided with claim forms and other records generated in the course of the insurance claim. Claim forms are completed by the claimant at the outset of the disability claim: they describe the nature and date of onset of the claimed disability, the nature of the claimant's occupation, and a description of the claimant's condition by the treating physician. Other documents may include periodic progress reports completed by the claimant and updated statements from the treating physician. There may also be memos documenting telephone conversations with the claimant, correspondence between the insurance company and the claimant, reviews by consultants, and other internal documentation.

Self-Report Data from the Claimant

Once the evaluator has had the opportunity to thoroughly review the written documentation, the evaluator should proceed with the face-to-face examination of the claimant. As described in Chapter 4, it is essential to obtain the claimant's informed consent before beginning any aspect of the examination. The evaluator should provide a detailed explanation about the circumstances and purpose of the evaluation. The evaluator should make clear her relationship with the referral source, the anticipated duration of the evaluation, the limits of confidentiality, and restrictions on the claimant's access to the results of the evaluation. The claimant should be given the opportunity to ask questions about the IME process and to express any concerns.

Since most IMEs take place when the claimant's disability status is being questioned, it is not unusual for claimants to approach the IME with a wary, hostile, or defensive attitude. Although, as with all forensic mental health evaluations, it should be made absolutely clear that the purpose is evaluative and not therapeutic, some effort should be directed toward developing a working rapport with the claimant. This can be facilitated by expressing a desire to understand the claimant's point of view, by emphasizing the evaluator's role as an independent fact-finder, and by treating the claimant in a professional and respectful manner.

5
chapter

The claimant should be oriented to the evaluator's office, given information about when and where breaks may be taken, shown the location of restrooms, and given other practical information.

Evaluations usually begin with an interview of the claimant, although some evaluators prefer to have the claimant complete questionnaires or some portions of the psychometric assessment at the beginning of the evaluation, prior to the interview. The advantage of the latter approach is that it allows the evaluator to review this information and inquire about areas of interest during the interview. Alternatively, the evaluator can complete the bulk of the interview prior to psychometric assessment and then follow up with additional questions after the completion of the testing.

Sufficient time should be allowed for an in-depth interview of the claimant. A thorough interview generally takes a minimum of two hours or three hours due to the breadth of information that should be covered. In addition to obtaining the claimant's point of view on his condition and impairments, this interview also provides the opportunity for the evaluator to observe the claimant's appearance, speech, affect, and behavior, as well as to make an informal assessment of his attention, concentration, and memory.

Given the amount of information that must be covered during the interview, it is important for the evaluator to maintain control of the structure of the interview. The interview should include a discussion of the claimant's history, information about the onset of her difficulties, and a discussion of her current situation. The interview should focus on obtaining detailed descriptive information about the claimant's functioning rather than asking the claim-

ant to provide definitive statements about her disability status. For example, the claimant could be asked to describe a typical day at work or to provide specific examples of how concentration problems affect her ability to manage household tasks.

In the course of the interview, the following topics should be addressed:

- *Social history*: Including the claimant's childhood, adolescence, adulthood, family structure, and marital/relationship history.

- *Educational history*: Academic and behavioral performance, beginning in elementary school, attitudes toward school, perceptions of successes and failures, history of participation in special education programs, identification of specific learning problems, class standing in high school and college, SAT or other standardized test scores, disciplinary actions, and referrals to the school psychologist or other professionals.

- *Occupational history*: How the claimant chose his career, any career changes, satisfaction and dissatisfaction with work, history of job losses or promotions, how often the claimant changed jobs and for what reasons.

- *Legal history*: Involvement with the criminal justice system, history of civil litigation (as plaintiff or as defendant), involvement in family court, restraining orders, or administrative actions (such as license revocation or suspension).

- *Medical history*: Current or past health problems, surgeries, hospitalizations, current and past medications, history of accidents or injuries, nature of current medical care.

- *Psychiatric history*: Inpatient and outpatient treatment for any psychiatric or behavioral problems (including marital, relationship, or family therapy), current and past psychotropic medications, nature and frequency of current and past psychotherapeutic treatment, reported diagnoses, attitude toward treatment.

5
chapter

- *Substance abuse history:* Use of alcohol, illegal drugs, abuse of prescription medications, history of substance abuse treatment, involvement in 12-Step or related programs, relapse history, his current status regarding use of drugs and alcohol.

- *Job duties:* Detailed description of duties, working conditions, schedule, and pace of work done just prior to the onset of her claimed disability.

- *Current daily activities:* How the claimant currently spends his day, involvement in activities of daily living, managing a household, care of children or other dependents, leisure activities, vacations taken, social activities, involvement in any "work-like" activities (e.g., reading professional journals, attending continuing education classes).

- *Disability onset:* Detailed description of the onset of the difficulties leading to her filing for disability benefits, including a description of the last day of work, her decision to leave work, her decision to seek treatment, and whether her decision to leave work was voluntary or mandated.

- *Functional impairments:* Detailed description of how his functioning has been affected by the reported condition, and any specific activities (work, social, home, leisure) that have been affected.

As previously noted, in addition to recording the claimant's verbal responses during the interview, the evaluator must also take careful note of the claimant's presentation and behaviors. During what is typically referred to as a "mental status examination," the evaluator should include observations about the claimant's appearance (including dress, posture, grooming, and hygiene), reported mood, affect, attitude, speech, thought processes, thought content (including orientation, concentration and attention, memory, abstraction,

BEST PRACTICE
Record detailed observations about the claimant's mental status.

fund of knowledge, and intelligence), judgment, insight, and receptive language.

In addition to the interview and observation described, self-report questionnaires and surveys can be useful for recording and documenting the claimant's reported symptoms, complaints, and functional limitations. Self-report questionnaires must be distinguished from psychological tests, in that the former were developed for clinical rather than forensic use, they have high face validity, and they lack the means for assessing the validity of the claimant's responses. Instruments falling into this category include social history forms, symptom checklists, and questionnaires regarding functional limitations.

As discussed in Chapter 3, the accuracy of self-reported data appears to be influenced by situational factors such as involvement in litigation or compensation-seeking (Lees-Haley et al., 1997; Williams et al., 1999). Specifically, in compensation situations, examinees are more likely to report superior premorbid functioning and poorer current functioning, and are more likely to exaggerate the number and severity of their symptoms (Williams et al., 1999). These tendencies need to be taken into consideration when evaluating the accuracy of the claimant's self-report.

Psychological Testing

Psychometric assessment is an integral component of the psychological IME. The ability to obtain and use test data allows psychologists to have the advantage of incorporating objective and subjective data that go beyond the observational and historical information available to other IME providers. This gives psychologists the benefit of having access to a greater breadth of data from which to formulate an opinion.

5
chapter

It is important to select tests carefully, keeping in mind the specific questions of the referral. In general, these questions address three areas of concern:

1. Does the claimant have a valid condition, and if so, what manifestations of the condition does the claimant experience?

2. How do the manifestations of the claimant's condition affect the claimant's functional capacity?

3. Do impairments in functioning limit the claimant's ability to perform the duties of the claimant's occupation?

Thus, assessment instruments should be selected that address one or more of these issues. Prior to beginning the IME, the evaluator must have some understanding of the condition, symptoms, and impairments the claimant is reporting. In addition, the evaluator must consider the types of impairments that are likely to affect the claimant's specific occupational duties. For example, if a claimant reports that anxiety causes her hands to tremble, this impairment would be of greater relevance if the claimant is employed as a neurosurgeon than if she is employed as an elementary school teacher. On the other hand, if the claimant reports that bipolar disorder results in unpredictable episodes of irritability, poor judgment, and impulsivity, these impairments would be relevant regardless of whether she is a surgeon or a teacher.

When contemplating the use of any particular test, there are several other factors the evaluator should consider:

- Is the test commercially published and peer-reviewed?

- Is the test reliable and valid for the purpose for which it will be used?

- Does the evaluator have the training, experience, and qualifications to administer and interpret the test?

- Is the test commonly used in forensic evaluations in general, and in IMEs in particular?

- Are there admissibility issues under *Frye* or *Daubert* standards?

BEST PRACTICE
Prior to conducting the evaluation, make sure you have some understanding of the claimant's reported condition, symptoms, and impairments, and how these impairments could affect the claimant's ability to perform his occupational duties.

In general, evaluators should avoid tests that are uncommon or obscure. Tests should never be used for other than their intended purposes, and standard administrative procedures must be followed. This means that all tests must be completed in the evaluator's office and under supervision. Under no circumstances should the claimant ever be given test materials to take home and complete. Table 5.2 provides a list of assessment instruments commonly used in disability evaluations.

Assessing Psychopathology

If the claimant is reporting disability as a result of a psychiatric condition, testing should be utilized that provides information helpful in determining the nature and severity of the claimant's condition and the symptoms he experiences. In choosing assessment instruments, it is important to recognize the differences between instruments designed for primarily for clinical purposes and those appropriate for forensic assessment. Multiscale personality inventories, such as the MMPI-2 (Butcher et al., 2001) and the PAI (Morey, 1991), are particularly useful. They include sophisticated validity scales for the detection of exaggerated or other distorted response sets, as well as facilitating an assessment of a broad range of psychopathology. There is a considerable research base supporting the use of these inventories in forensic settings. The inclusion of either the MMPI-2 or the PAI in an IME is strongly recommended.

In some cases, the evaluator may want to use additional instruments to obtain further information about the claimant's specific condition. For example, the Trauma Symptom Inventory (TSI, Briere, 1995) might be utilized for claims of disability related to PTSD, or the Millon Clinical Multiaxial Inventory-III (MCMI-III, Millon et al., 2006) might be helpful when a personality disorder is suspected. It should be remembered, however, that these instruments were designed for clinical assessment. As such, these instruments should not be a primary basis for decision-making in an IME, but should be regarded as supplemental sources of data only.

As mentioned earlier in this chapter, symptom checklists, such as the Beck Depression Inventory (Beck, 1987), Beck Anxiety Inventory (Beck & Steer, 1990), and Symptom Checklist–90, (Derogatis, 1977) may provide a useful format for collecting

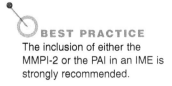

BEST PRACTICE
The inclusion of either the MMPI-2 or the PAI in an IME is strongly recommended.

Table 5.2 | Suggestions for Test Selection

To assess condition:	Psychopathology	Psychopathology with cognitive screening	Cognitive disorder

	• Choose one of these:
	  ○ MMPI-2
	  ○ PAI
	• Optional (if needed):
	  ○ Condition- specific instruments (e.g. TSI, MCMI-III)
		• Choose one of these:
		  ○ MMPI-2
		  ○ PAI
		• And one of these:
		  ○ Neuropsychological screening instrument (e.g., RBANS)
		  ○ WAIS-IV + WMS-IV
		• Optional (if needed):
		  ○ Condition-specific instruments (e.g., TSI, MCMI-III)
			• Perform a full neuropsychological assessment of these domains:
			  ○ Intelligence
			  ○ Academic
			  ○ Executive functions
			  ○ Attention
			  ○ Concentration
			  ○ Processing speed
			  ○ Language
			  ○ Visual-spatial
			  ○ Motor
			  ○ Sensory
			  ○ Learning
			  ○ Memory
			• And choose one of these:
			  ○ MMPI-2
			  ○ PAI

To assess response style:

- Choose one of these:
  - MMPI-2: F-family scales + FBS + RBS
  - PAI: NIM
- And one of these:
  - SIRS-2
  - M-FAST
  - SIMS
  - MPS

- Choose one of these:
  - MMPI-2: F-family scales + FBS + RBS
  - PAI: NIM
- And one of these:
  - SIRS-2
  - M-FAST
  - SIMS
  - MPS
- And one of these:
  - VIP
  - CARB
  - TOMM
  - WMT

- Choose two of these:
  - VIP
  - CARB
  - TOMM
  - WMT
- And choose one of these:
  - MMPI-2: F-family scales + FBS + RBS
  - PAI: NIM

the claimant's self-report. Because of this, the evaluator may wish to include such questionnaires in the IME. However, given their high face-validity and lack of validity scales, these instruments are not appropriate for drawing definitive conclusions regarding the presence of valid symptoms.

In general, the use of projective techniques, such as the Rorschach (Rorschach, 1921) and the Thematic Apperception Test (Murray, 1943), is not recommended. Although these techniques may yield interesting clinical data that could be helpful in a treatment setting, their usefulness in an assessment of disability has not been established. In addition, these techniques may face admissibility challenges in some jurisdictions. Projective techniques are time-consuming to administer and interpret. Given the relatively limited time available for data collection in an IME, the evaluator's time would be better spent on other tasks.

Assessing Cognitive Functioning

Evaluators may be asked to assess the claimant's cognitive functioning in a variety of circumstances, ranging from a brief screening to rule out impairments in memory or concentration, to a complete neuropsychological assessment battery. Alleged cognitive impairments may be attributed to a variety of causes, including psychiatric conditions such as depression, anxiety, or post-traumatic stress disorder; long-term substance abuse; traumatic brain injury; organic brain disorders; or medical conditions. Although some elements of cognitive functioning can be appropriately assessed by clinical psychologists, it is critical that the evaluator not exceed her level of competence in assessing cognitive functioning. Full neuropsychological assessment batteries should not be undertaken by psychologists who have not had formal education, training, and experience in conducting these assessments. Full batteries typically include assessments of intelligence, academic achievement, executive functions, attention and concentration, processing speed, language, visual-spatial skills, motor functioning, sensory functioning, learning, and memory.

BEWARE
Do not undertake to perform a full neuropsychological evaluation unless you have had adequate training, education, and experience in neuropsychology.

In some cases, when doing an assessment of psychopathology, the evaluator may be asked to perform a "cognitive screening" as part of the IME. The purpose of cognitive screening is to rule out the presence of gross neuropsychological impairments. In this case, a full neuropsychological battery is not called for. Depending on the specific referral questions, the evaluator may choose to do an assessment of the claimant's intellectual functioning and his memory (i.e., WAIS and WMS) or may elect to use a screening instrument such as the Repeatable Battery for the Assessment of Neuropsychological Status (RBANS, Randolph, 1998). In any case, the evaluator must be clear that a cognitive screening is not equivalent to a comprehensive neuropsychological battery in terms of scope and detail.

Whether the evaluator is being asked to perform a limited assessment of cognitive functioning or a comprehensive battery, his selection of appropriate instruments is critical. It is usually inappropriate to utilize abbreviated versions of instruments, to substitute screening instruments for a battery of tests when a comprehensive assessment is requested, to use outdated versions of instruments, and to use instruments that have not been validated for the purpose or population in question.

Assessing Response Style

A formal assessment of the claimant's response style should be an integral part of the IME. As noted in Chapter 3, although the specific base rate of malingering in disability evaluations is unknown, estimates range from 7.5% to 33% of claims (Samuel & Mittenberg, 2005). A variety of instruments to assess symptom validity is available. Selection should be made by considering the nature of the claimant's reported symptoms, the appropriateness of the instrument for the population, and the psychometric properties of the instrument. Rogers and Payne (2006) noted, "In the case of feigned mental disorders, the malingerer must create a believable set of symptoms, a likely onset and course of the disorder, and plausible effects on their day-to-day functioning." On the other hand, feigning a cognitive disorder requires "effortful failure"—that is, "While appearing invested in succeeding, [the claimant reports] incorrect responses on test items that measure cognitive abilities." Thus, the approaches used to assess malingered psychopathology and feigned cognitive symptoms are quite different.

Psychometric approaches to assessing the authenticity of psychiatric symptoms typically compare the examinee's portrayal of the nature and severity of her symptoms to what is known about the course of valid psychiatric conditions. When the symptoms reported by the examinee are bizarre, extremely severe, incongruous, and/or inconsistent, questions regarding the validity of these symptoms are raised.

Both the MMPI-2 and the PAI include scales to assess the validity of the examinee's responses. On the MMPI-2, the so called "F-family" scales (F, Fb, F_p) are composed of items infrequently endorsed by normative samples (F, Fb) or by psychiatric inpatient samples (F_p). The interpretation of these scales is based on the theory that over-endorsement of unusual symptoms may be a sign of malingering. Items composing these scales tend to include bizarre and extreme symptoms. The Fake Bad Scale (Lees-Haley et al., 1991) items were rationally derived. The FBS was designed to detect non-credible symptom presentations as expressed in litigation settings, particularly somatic and/or non-psychotic symptoms. The recently developed Response Bias Scale (Gervais et al. 2007) was empirically derived by identifying MMPI-2 items that were differentially endorsed by individuals passing or failing the Word Memory Test (Green, 2003). On the PAI, the Negative Impression Management scale (NIM) is based on items infrequently endorsed by normative and patient samples.

Structured interviews are another approach to assessing symptom validity. These include the Structured

INFO

Assessment methods for determining the validity of reported symptoms fall into three categories:

● scales imbedded within other assessment instruments
● structured interviews
● paper and pencil tests

Inventory of Reported Symptoms 2nd edition (Rogers et al., 2010) and the Miller Forensic Assessment of Symptoms Test (Miller, 2001). Both of these instruments are designed specifically to assess feigning of psychiatric symptoms. The SIRS-2 employs a variety of detection strategies, including rare symptoms, improbable symptoms, symptom combinations, symptom severity, indiscriminate symptom endorsement, obvious versus subtle symptoms, erroneous stereotypes, and reported versus observed symptoms. The SIRS-2 consists of 172 items and takes approximately an hour to administer. The M-FAST is described as a screening instrument. It consists of 25 items and can be administered in five to ten minutes. M-FAST scales include Reported vs. Observed (symptoms) (RO), Extreme Symptomatology (ES), Rare Combinations (RC), Unusual Hallucinations (UH), Unusual Symptom Course (USC), Negative Image (NI), and Suggestibility (ES).

The Structured Inventory of Malingered Symptoms (Widows & Smith, 2005) and the Malingering Probability Scale (MPS, Silverton & Gruber, 1998) are paper-and-pencil tests. The SIMS is described as a screening measure for malingered psychopathology and cognitive symptoms. Consisting of 75 items, the SIMS takes 10 to 15 minutes to complete. Test items were constructed from a combination of revised validity questions from existing instruments and characteristics of malingerers noted by existing research. The MPS consists of 139 true–false items and can be completed in 20 minutes. MPS scales for post-traumatic stress, schizophrenia, depression, and dissociative disorders address real psychopathology, while a large set of parallel items represents simulated psychopathology. This non-overlapping subset of "pseudo" symptoms is the basis for discriminating between honest and dishonest protocols.

Approaches to detecting feigned cognitive deficits differ from the methods used to evaluate the validity of psychiatric symptoms. Cognitive feigning typically involves the examinee's performing at a sub-maximal level. He may accomplish this by deliberately giving incorrect answers, by failing to give his full attention to tasks, by making careless or random responses, or by intentionally working at a slower pace. The result is a test score that does not reflect the examinee's true ability.

5
chapter

Numerous instruments are available to assess the validity of cognitive symptoms. The Test of Memory Malingering (Tombaugh, 1996) is a 50-item picture-recognition test designed to discriminate between malingered and true memory impairments. The TOMM consists of two learning trials and an optional retention trial. Like the TOMM, the Victoria Symptom Validity Test (Slick et al., 1997) and the Computerized Assessment of Response Bias (Allen et al., 1997) use a forced-choice format. Both the VSVT and the CARB are computer-administered, visually presented digit-recognition procedures. The Word Memory Test (Green 2003) is a forced-choice verbal memory task. Finally, the Validity Indicator Profile (Frederick, 1997) uses a forced-choice format, but unlike the other instruments mentioned above, the VIP is not presented to the examinee as a memory test. The VIP is composed of both verbal and nonverbal subtests. Based on her performance on the VIP, the examinee's response style is classified as compliant, inconsistent, irrelevant, or suppressed.

Collateral Interviews

Collaterals, such as treatment providers, family members, and professional associates, can provide valuable data regarding the claimant's condition and functional capacity. The evaluator should make a concerted effort to identify and obtain information from appropriate collateral sources during the course of the evaluation. During the interview and while reviewing written records, the evaluator should begin to think about which sources are likely to be useful and could help clarify critical issues. Once the potential collaterals have been identified, the evaluator must seek written authorization from the claimant before contacting these individuals.

The purpose of a collateral interview is not to obtain the collateral's opinion about the claimant's disability status, but to gather relevant observational data from the collateral's perspective. There are no standard instruments for collecting data or observations from collaterals regarding disability

BEST PRACTICE
You must obtain written permission from the claimant before contacting individuals for collateral interviews.

issues; therefore, the evaluator should develop questions for each interview in advance. As with claimant interviews, information is best solicited with open-ended questions about the collateral's observations of the claimant. The collateral should then be asked to provide specific examples to support his general statements. For example, if the claimant's spouse reports that the she "can't do anything around the house," he could be asked to provide details regarding the particular tasks that the claimant is no longer able to do. Collaterals should never be asked to offer conclusive statements about the claimant's disability status.

Collateral information can be obtained in a number of ways, including telephone interviews, face-to-face interviews, and written responses to questions. Telephone interviews are usually the most efficient method. After obtaining authorization from the claimant, the evaluator should contact the collateral to arrange a time for the interview. Allowing 30 to 60 minutes is usually sufficient for a collateral interview. Although the evaluator does not need to obtain written authorization from the collateral, the evaluator should clearly inform the collateral about the purpose and context of the interview, the intended use of the material, that the collateral's participation is voluntary, the limits of confidentiality, and the fact that the information given will be attributed to the source.

As noted earlier, many different individuals can provide collateral information about the claimant. It is unlikely that the evaluator will be able to interview every possible source. From a practical standpoint, IMEs usually include between one and three collateral sources. When selecting collateral sources, the following factors should be considered:

- How much access has the collateral had to the claimant? What is the nature of the access? What behaviors would the collateral have had the opportunity to observe?

- What degree of objectivity can be expected from the collateral? Does the collateral have a vested interest in the outcome of the evaluation? Is the collateral subject to other conscious or unconscious influences that might bias the collateral's point of view?

- Does the collateral possess expertise relevant to the information being sought? How knowledgeable is the collateral likely to be about the subjects being discussed?

- Was the methodology utilized by the collateral to obtain the data reliable? Is the collateral's information based on firsthand knowledge or was it obtained in some other way?

- Is the collateral likely to provide unique information that cannot be obtained from other sources?

Collateral sources can be individuals who have treated the claim-ant, who live with or know the claimant personally, or who have known the claimant through the claimant's work (see Table 5.3). The ideal collateral source is someone who has had ample opportunity to observe relevant dimensions of the claimant's behavior,

Table 5.3 | Possible Sources of Collateral Information

Treatment Providers	Personal Associates	Professional Associates
Current psychotherapist	Spouse	Coworker
Current psychiatrist	Significant Other	Business Partner
Primary Care Physician	Sibling	Professional Colleague
Medical Specialist	Parent	Supervisor
Former psychotherapist	Other family members	Customer or Client
Former psychiatrist	Neighbors	
	Friends	

who is objective and unbiased, and who can communicate these observations effectively and accurately. Rarely is such an individual available to the evaluator. Thus it is usually beneficial to seek information from two or more collaterals, each of whom has had the opportunity to observe different aspects of the claimant's behavior.

Treatment Providers

Psychiatrists, psychologists, and psychotherapists are the most commonly used collateral sources in IMEs. As collaterals, treatment providers have a number of advantages. As professionals, treatment providers often have extensive training and experience in diagnosing and treating individuals with mental health issues. They are in a position to assess the claimant's condition over time and the claimant's response to treatment. They are knowledgeable about diagnosis and associated signs and symptoms of various conditions. They have been privy to the patient's personal disclosures.

Despite these advantages, the evaluator should be mindful that a treating provider knows the claimant in the context of a therapeutic relationship. As noted by Greenberg and Shuman (1997), there are several key differences between therapeutic and forensic roles. A therapist demonstrates support, acceptance, and empathy toward the patient and seeks to understand his perceptions and feelings. The therapist's knowledge of the patient's world is usually based exclusively on the patient's self-report, and thus is likely to be skewed by his biases, assumptions, and attitudes. The therapist is less concerned about the objective truth of the patient's circumstances than in the patient's subjective understanding of these circumstances. Thus, the therapist's view of the patient's situation is unavoidably influenced by these factors. This tendency must be taken into consideration when evaluating information obtained from treatment providers.

Typical issues to discuss with treatment providers during a collateral interview include the following:

- When treatment began, and how the claimant was referred to the provider.

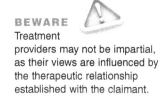

BEWARE Treatment providers may not be impartial, as their views are influenced by the therapeutic relationship established with the claimant.

5 chapter

- The nature and frequency of the treatment.

- The provider's diagnostic impression, and the signs and symptoms observed by the provider to support her diagnosis.

- Whether the provider knew the claimant prior to the onset of the disability claim and how the claimant's condition has changed over time.

- The claimant's investment in, response to, and compliance with treatment.

- Whether the claimant's reported impairments (e.g., poor memory, mood instability) have been directly observed by the provider.

- If the provider believes the claimant cannot or should not return to work; the specific reasons for this conclusion.

- Whether the claimant has been referred for additional or adjunctive treatment (e.g., medication evaluation, inpatient hospitalization, neuropsychological evaluation), and the claimant's response to these suggestions.

- The provider's understanding of the claimant's former work duties.

- The provider's understanding of the claimant's current daily activities.

- Whether the provider encouraged or recommended that the claimant apply for disability benefits.

Personal Associates

The claimant's spouse and family members usually know the claimant most intimately. Unlike a therapist, who may spend an hour each week with the claimant, family members are with the claimant day in and day out. They have had the opportunity to observe the claimant over the course of time in diverse situations and circumstances.

The obvious downside to this, however, is that by virtue of these close relationships, family members are unlikely to be objective observers of the claimant. Multiple and complex influences may affect the relationship between the family members and the claimant. As noted by Heilbrun, Warren, and Picarello (2003), "Many individuals who might be interviewed . . . are not impartial; they may have strong feelings about the individual being evaluated and an associated wish for a certain kind of outcome . . ." (p. 83). This is certainly true in the case of family members who may, for example, be angry with the claimant for leaving work, or who, conversely, may be depending on his disability benefits for financial support. Family members may also be concerned about the consequences of disclosures to the evaluator in terms of their relationship with the claimant, especially when the information they provide may contribute to the discontinuation of his benefits.

Typical issues to discuss with personal associates include the following:

- Changes they have noticed in the claimant's behavior, when these changes occurred, and how they became aware of these changes.
- The claimant's current daily activities. How she spends each day.
- Specific impairments in the claimant's functioning they have observed.
- Changes in the claimant's performance of household responsibilities and how family members have compensated for this.
- Changes in her social, travel, and leisure activities.
- The claimant's ability to perform activities of daily living, including self-care.
- The claimant's behavior at family gatherings and holidays.
- How family relationships have been affected by the claimant's condition.
- Whether treatment has been helpful to the claimant. Changes they have observed since she began treatment.

5
chapter

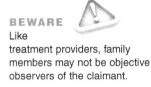

Professional Associates

Individuals who have had the opportunity to observe the claimant's functioning at work have the potential to provide extremely useful data. This is especially true of individuals who have known the claimant for a number of years and can describe his behavior before the onset of the disability claim. Depending on the nature of the claimant's occupation and work setting, collaterals could include coworkers, associates, colleagues, supervisors, business partners, assistants, clients, and customers. Professional associates may have the advantage of being less personally involved with the claimant than family members, and, therefore, somewhat more objective. That said, it is important not to discount the possible influence of external factors or personal concerns on the part of professional associates. Factors such as competition, fear of reprisal, exposure to litigation, loyalty, financial gain, and rivalry may affect the objectivity and candor of the collateral's responses.

Typical issues to discuss with professional associates include:

- Observed changes in the claimant's behavior at work.
- The specific job duties and tasks that were affected by his condition.
- How the quality, consistency, and/or pace of his work was affected.
- Whether he made serious errors at work.
- Whether others voiced concerns about the claimant's condition and behavior.
- If the claimant suffered any measurable external consequences as a result of these difficulties (e.g., loss of license, legal action, loss of business).

Conclusion

The importance of careful and comprehensive data collection cannot be overemphasized. The selection of appropriate data sources should be guided by the specific referral questions the evaluator is being asked to address. The use of multiple data sources is strongly recommended to provide a solid foundation for the evaluator's conclusions. Typical data sources include written records, self-report information from the claimant, psychometric test data, and information obtained from collateral sources. Each of these sources has specific assets and limitations, which must be taken into consideration by the evaluator.

5
chapter

Data Interpretation | **6**

The previous two chapters were devoted to planning and performing the evaluation. The task now shifts to analyzing and interpreting the evaluation data so the evaluator can respond to the referral questions. Data interpretation requires an orderly, methodical approach, consistent with the scientific method (see adjacent information box).

Step One: Identify Hypotheses

Developing hypotheses is a cornerstone of the scientific method. Hypotheses form the basis and structure for data interpretation. This is especially important in a complex evaluation, such as in a disability case. Interpreting the vast amount of data from multiple (and often conflicting) sources would create an overwhelming and unwieldy task without the structure of hypotheses to organize these data.

Grisso (2003) described the importance of forming causal hypotheses to help the finder of-fact weigh the plausibility of various explanations for the behavior in question and subsequently "collect and synthesize information that will test these hypotheses" (p. 476).

A simplistic approach to a disability evaluation would be to postulate a single hypothesis: *The claimant is (or is not) disabled.* The data analysis would then proceed to confirm or disconfirm this hypothesis.

INFO

Four steps of data interpretation:

1. Identify hypotheses

2. Organize data

3. Assess data

4. Form opinions

As has been noted before in this text, *disability* in this context is a legally defined term. As such, the specific question of "disability" should not be addressed at all by the evaluator. Rather, the questions to be addressed concern the claimant's condition and functional capacities, and the nexus between these and the demands of the claimant's job. Thus, an array of hypotheses is required to address the complex layers of this task. Although by no means exclusive, the following four hypotheses are offered as one way to approach this process. The evaluator will subsequently have the task of determining which of these hypotheses best fits the data that have been collected.

Hypothesis 1: The claimant does not have a genuine clinical condition.

As explained in Chapter 1, definitions of disability have two prongs: first, that the claimant has an illness or injury; and second, that the claimant's ability to work is compromised as a result. Thus, the existence of an illness or injury (i.e., "condition") must be confirmed or disconfirmed through the evaluation. In all but the most unusual cases, the claimant is asserting that he is clinically impaired. This assertion also may be endorsed by the claimant's treatment providers, employer, family members, and others. This cannot, however, simply be accepted at face value. The evaluator's task is to collect objective data to address this issue.

In addition to malingering, there are many situations in which, despite assertions to the contrary, the claimant does not actually have a genuine clinical condition. For example, she may be experiencing valid symptoms, but these symptoms do not constitute a "condition." Instead, these symptoms are normal variations of mood or functioning. A claimant may complain of forgetfulness that is actually due to normal

BEST PRACTICE

Be sure to formulate hypotheses to guide in the interpretation of data. For example:

1. The claimant does not have a genuine clinical condition.

2. The claimant has a genuine condition, but no functional impairments that interfere with her ability to work.

3. The claimant has a genuine clinical condition with functional impairments that interfere with the claimant's ability to perform his or her job.

4. The claimant is unable to perform her work duties for reasons not related to illness or injury.

age-related memory changes rather than to a cognitive disorder. A claimant may feel anxious after hearing about layoffs at work, but these symptoms are too circumscribed or transitory to constitute an anxiety disorder. Personality traits may also contribute to an individual's tendency to unconsciously magnify distress or seek external assistance and caretaking. There may be changes in her job responsibilities, such that the claimant is suddenly being asked to perform more difficult or complex tasks, leading her to conclude that there must be "something wrong" with her.

Hypothesis 2: The claimant has a genuine clinical condition, but has no functional impairments that interfere with the claimant's ability to work.

It is important to remember that not all conditions necessarily cause functional impairments. While any disorder conceivably can cause functional impairments, there is not necessarily a relationship between a condition and such functional impairment. Most conditions do result in some degree of impaired functioning. However, not all impairments interfere with work performance. Moreover, impairments that interfere with the performance of one job might not affect the performance of a different job. Thus, identifying the functional abilities required for the claimant's specific occupation is very important. Due to the nature of the claimant's job, some functional impairments may be irrelevant while others may be critical to his job performance. For example, consider functional abilities related to visual-spatial perception. Impairments in this area would affect the occupational functioning of a surgeon much more than that of an accountant.

Hypothesis 3: The claimant has a genuine clinical condition with functional impairments that interfere with the claimant's ability to perform her job.

Sometimes there are impairments that affect some elements of the claimant's work capacity, but do not completely preclude her occupational functioning. Most occupations are composed of more than one substantial and material job duty and require a

6
chapter

variety of functional abilities. Some of these abilities are essential; others, less so. There may be some aspects of the claimant's job functioning that are compromised, while other abilities remain intact. Sometimes impairments diminish the number of hours per day or days per week that a claimant can work, yet the claimant can function normally at other times.

When the claimant cannot accomplish the important substantial and material duties of his occupation due to impaired functioning, work performance becomes impossible. Consider, for example, a teacher with panic disorder who cannot tolerate being around people, or a stockbroker with rapid-cycling bipolar disorder who frequently makes irrational and impulsive financial decisions. These impairments interfere with such key aspects of their jobs that it is not possible for them to continue working. Note that every functional ability need not be affected in order for a claimant to be unable to perform her occupation. However, when critical elements (i.e., the substantial and material duties) can no longer be performed, even if the claimant can perform other aspects of the job, she would be unable to work. So if a teacher is unable to tolerate being around groups of students, it does not matter that she is able to plan lessons or calculate grades accurately. Teachers who cannot be around students cannot teach.

Hypothesis 4: The claimant is unable to perform his substantial and material occupational duties for reasons not related to an illness or injury.

Finally, circumstances unrelated to a condition may compromise or prevent work functioning. Examples of these situations include a lawyer who is disbarred due to financial misconduct, a business owner whose company goes broke because of unfavorable economic conditions, an executive who does not get along with the boss and is fired, and a doctor whose practice drops off after negative publicity related to a malpractice case. Sometimes there may be changes in the work environment, such as the installation of a new computer system, or an increase in workload that interferes with the claimant's ability to do her job. While work performance may be compromised in all these cases, this impairment cannot be attributed to an illness or injury.

Step Two: Organize Data

The second task in the process of data interpretation is to organize the data in a meaningful way to facilitate further analysis.

Time

Evaluation data can be organized in terms of the time period addressed. Because "disability" refers to a change in functional capacity, it is necessary to have an understanding of the claimant's functioning both before and after the onset of the claimed disability. The claimant's prior functioning is referred to as "baseline functioning." Ultimately, comparisons must be drawn between his baseline and current functioning in order to ascertain if there has been a notable decrement in his functional capacity coinciding with the disability claim. Knowledge of baseline functioning should be developed from objective rather than subjective (especially self-report) data. This can best be accomplished by comparing contemporaneous documentation from different time periods.

Sources of Information

Evaluation data can be organized by source of information. It is essential to know the source of the information when attempting to analyze conflicting data, as will be discussed in detail in the next section. The sources of data in a disability evaluation include, among other things, information obtained from self-report, treating professionals, collateral interviews, investigative reports, other written documentation such as employment and medical records, psychological and neuropsychological test data, and direct observation. Some of these categories can be further subdivided by the specific sources. So, for example, in terms of treating professionals, subcategories might include the treating psychiatrist, the psychotherapist, the primary care physician, and so on.

Functional Abilities

Perhaps the most important dimension in organizing evaluation data is by functional ability. Ideally, the relevant functional abilities were identified early in the evaluation. As was discussed in Chapter 2, functional abilities are, in a sense, the building blocks that underlie the performance of much more complex endeavors. Consider the occupation of a waiter, for example. It is composed of a number of job duties. Some of these job duties are very important (i.e., "substantial and material"), such as taking orders from diners, communicating orders to the kitchen, and delivering food to diners. Other duties, such as making pleasant small talk with diners, are more peripheral and less essential. Each of these job duties is composed of functional abilities necessary for the performance of the task. For example, "taking orders from diners" requires being able to hear and understand verbal information, respond verbally to questions, accurately record information in writing, and work at an appropriate pace and speed.

The evaluator must identify the specific functional abilities necessary for the performance of the substantial and material duties of the claimant's occupation to determine if the claimant's work capacity is compromised. To prevent the evaluation and data analysis from becoming too unwieldy, the evaluator should focus on the most important duties of the claimant's occupation and the most important functional abilities that relate to those duties. There is likely to be some overlap of functional abilities among job duties. The evaluator must be sure to collect data addressing each of these functional abilities.

Conceptualizing the Overall Schema

The three dimensions of data organization just described can be combined into a matrix. Although creating a three-dimensional model is possible, it is more difficult to conceptualize and does not lend itself well to data analysis. Instead, create two matrices: one addressing baseline functioning and the second addressing current functioning.

As illustrated in the simplified example shown in Tables 6.1 and 6.2, the horizontal axis lists functional abilities, and the vertical axis lists sources of data.

Each cell would be completed by adding the relevant data obtained in the course of the evaluation. Obviously, not every cell in the grid will be filled, as not each source of information will address each functional ability. The example here shows a partial grid as completed for a claimant employed as a middle-school teacher.

Organizing the evaluation data in this manner facilitates data analysis by allowing cross-source comparison of information regarding particular functional abilities. This helps the evaluator identify areas where there is convergence or divergence between data sources. This also facilitates comparisons between the claimant's baseline functioning and his current functioning. Finally, it ensures that key pieces of data, especially conflicting data, will not be overlooked.

> **BEST PRACTICE**
> Data can be organized into matrices. Create one matrix to address baseline functioning and another to address current functioning

Step Three: Assess Data

To serve as a basis for accurate inferences, the data underlying these inferences must be valid and relevant. The importance of this

Table 6.1 | Baseline or Current Functioning

	Functional Ability	Functional Ability	Functional Ability
Data Source			
Data Source			
Data Source			

Table 6.2 | Current Functioning

	Keep accurate written records	**Maintain emotional control**	**Sustain focus and attention**
Self-report	"I make mistakes calculating grades"	"I started crying in the middle of a lesson"	"I lose track of what people are saying to me"
Psychometric testing	WAIS: VIQ = 103, PSI = 83	MMPI-2: Elevations on Scales 2 and 7	WMS: Logical Memory Scale score = 13
Treating psychotherapist	"She wrote me a check for $1000 instead of $10"	"Cries frequently during sessions"	"Seems very attentive during therapy"

in terms of legal admissibility standards is embodied in the Federal Rules of Evidence, Rule 702, Testimony by Experts:

> If scientific, technical, or other specialized knowledge will assist the trier of fact to understand the evidence or to determine a fact in issue, a witness qualified as an expert by knowledge, skill, experience, training, or education, may testify thereto in the form of an opinion or otherwise, if (1) the testimony is based upon sufficient facts or data, (2) the testimony is the product of reliable principles and methods, and (3) the witness has applied the principles and methods reliably to the facts of the case.

As noted earlier in this chapter, a typical disability evaluation will yield a complex array of data. Although some of these data will fall neatly into place, other data will present an inconsistent or contradictory picture. Thus, the evaluator must coalesce, weigh, and interpret these data in order to test hypotheses and formulate opinions. In order to accomplish this, each piece of information must be evaluated to determine its validity and relevance to the referral questions. Employing a flawed methodology can lead to unreliable data. In the case of disability, the evaluator typically obtains data through direct observation of and interaction with the claimant, the results of psychometric testing, and information obtained from third-party sources. As described in earlier chapters, these data should be collected in a predetermined, systematic manner. Despite this, the evaluator should always scrutinize the underlying methodologies when reviewing and analyzing the evaluation data.

Self-Report Data

Heilbrun (2001) noted that one of the more important distinctions between a forensic assessment and a therapeutic assessment is the presumed accuracy of the self-report of the individual being evaluated. The term *dissimulation* refers to the intentional misrepresentation of symptoms and functional deficits in order to obtain a desired result. This includes efforts to minimize symptoms as well as efforts to exaggerate symptoms. In the context of a disability evaluation, dissimulation, when present, usually involves the exaggeration of symptoms and the degree of impairment.

It is critical that the evaluator take steps to assess the credibility of the claimant's self-report. The presumed base rate of malingering in disability evaluations is significant. Samuel and Mittenberg (2005) report that malingering is estimated to occur in 7.5% to 33% of disability claimants. Dissimulation, however, is not limited to malingering. Rogers and Payne (2006) discuss three categories of dissimulation relevant to disability evaluations: (a) the malingering of symptoms and associated features, (b) false claims that legitimate symptoms directly arose from a compensable condition, and (c) faked impairment for genuine symptoms. Exaggeration or magnification of symptoms occurs more frequently than complete faking of illness or injury (Gold et al., 2008).

Assessment of malingering should not be taken lightly. Gold and colleagues (2008) warn that an implication of malingering can have serious consequences for the claimant, and therefore, the determination should be based on convincing evidence. There appears to be a consensus in the literature that the best way to approach this is by comparing information from a variety of

BEWARE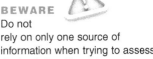
Do not
rely on only one source of
information when trying to assess
dissimulation. Consider
information from a variety of
sources.

sources, such as interviews with claimants, treatment providers, family members, and co-workers; clinical records; psychological test reports; investigations; and work reports. (See, for example, Gold et al., 2008; Heilbrun, 2002; Rogers & Payne, 2006; Samuel & Mittenberg, 2005; Sreenivasan et al., 2003; Rogers & Bender, 2003). A determination of malingering should never be based on psychometric testing alone.

Several approaches for systematically investigating dissimulation have been suggested. Sreenivasan and colleagues propose an assessment guide consisting of consideration of neuropsychological (or psychological)testing issues, congruence of testing and behavior, congruence of symptoms or signs with clinical data, and non-clinical factors. Similarly, Samuel and Mittenberg advise considering symptoms and features in four domains: (1) motivation/circumstances (e.g., financial incentives, work-related problems, legal problems); (2) symptoms (e.g., atypical symptoms, exaggerated symptoms, incongruent symptoms); (3) claimant interview presentation (e.g., discrepancies, lack of cooperation, admission of malingering); and (4) activity or behavior outside the interview (e.g., noncompliance with treatment, impairments affect only work, capacity for recreation). These authors also identified factors that, when present, argue against the presence of malingering. These included: participation in aggressive treatment; well-documented, objective evidence of symptoms and problems prior to the claim of disability; obvious losses of a significant nature; and presence of behavior or symptoms that are self-defeating rather than self-aggrandizing.

The presence of symptom-exaggeration does not preclude the simultaneous existence of a valid condition. Some claimants exaggerate the severity of their difficulties in order to ensure that they will be taken seriously. Even when claimants intentionally feign certain symptoms, there may be other (genuine) symptoms, either at a less severe level or of an entirely different nature, that are present. For example, a claimant may feign depression, but may actually experience genuine cognitive deficits such as memory loss.

A claimant's self-report may be inaccurate for reasons other than malingering. Some claimants are excessively influenced by family members or treatment providers who believe the claimant is more limited than is actually the case. Other claimants may be predisposed to take a very pessimistic view of their abilities or prognoses. At times, the nature of the claimant's condition can affect the quality of her self-report. People with depression, for example, tend to be less hopeful and less confident than people without depression. The claimant might communicate incorrect information unknowingly or unintentionally. For example, a claimant may report that he was fired because of psychological problems, when in fact the termination was due to economic factors.

BEST PRACTICE
Suggestions for analyzing self-report data:

- Investigate dissimulation in every evaluation.

- Compare data from multiple sources.

- Incorporate data from psychometric testing, including inspection of validity scales, overall patterns, and symptom validity measures.

- Do not assume that malingering precludes the existence of actual symptoms and deficits.

- Consider other forms of distortion that may be unconscious or unintended.

Third-Party Data

Third-party data, in the form of written records or direct interviews, are a key component in any forensic evaluation. They allow the evaluator to "cross-validate" information obtained from the claimant and from psychometric assessment, thus increasing the degree of confidence in the evaluator's conclusions. Third-party data, however, are just as vulnerable to distortion and misinterpretation as any other form of evaluation data.

In terms of bias, the third-party source, like the claimant, may have a "vested interest" in the outcome of the evaluation. Family members may be depending on disability benefits for financial support. Treatment providers may wish to support their patients. Employers may see a disability claim as an opportunity to be rid of a difficult employee. Influences such as these can affect the information

INFO

According to Heilbrun (2002), the following four factors may affect third-party data:

1. bias
2. expertise
3. suggestibility
4. memory loss

reported by the source. This reinforces the importance of using multiple sources for third-party information in order to counteract the bias of any particular source.

The expertise of the source can also affect the nature of the information provided. Individuals who lack training and experience in psychopathology may misinterpret the claimant's behavior, either failing to recognize subtle indicators of clinical disturbance, or misjudging normal variations of mood or behavior as signs of psychiatric difficulties. Information from investigators, insurance company personnel, and family members may contain inaccurate conclusions like these due to lack of expertise. Thus, it is particularly important to elicit descriptions rather than conclusions when the expertise of the source is limited.

Suggestibility occurs when third-party sources are influenced by the manner in which questions are being asked. Opening with questions such as, "When did you first notice he was depressed?" implies that depression is present. This assumption will influence the answers to subsequent questions. Heilbrun (2002) suggests beginning a third-party interview with very general questions before proceeding to more specific areas, to avoid contaminating the source's information with leading questions.

Possible memory loss is another factor that must be taken into consideration with third-party sources. This is especially relevant when the source is being questioned about prior events or circumstances. Examples of this include questions about the claimant's academic, psychological, or medical functioning prior to the onset of the disability claim. The risk of inaccurate recollection is even greater when the data in question were not recorded in some fashion contemporaneously. For this reason, when dealing with prior events, it is usually more helpful to rely on written records from the time period in question, such as hospital records or school transcripts, rather than the recollection of individuals.

In addition to the factors discussed by Heilbrun, two additional factors can influence third-party data. As with other sources of data, the validity of third-party data can be compromised by errors in observation, interpretation, reporting, and recording. A third-party source may incorrectly observe a given behavior or may interpret the observed behavior erroneously. Trembling, for example, may be incorrectly attributed to anxiety rather than a medical condition. Errors can occur in the reporting of data. Sources may unknowingly

BEST PRACTICE

Suggestions for analyzing third-party data are as follows:

- Compare information across sources.

- Focus on descriptive information rather than conclusions.

- Consider the information available to the source, the source's expertise, potential bias, and the source's methodology in obtaining and recording the data.

- Ensure that written records are not misinterpreted due to illegibility or factual errors.

and unintentionally communicate incorrect information. Investigative reports may incorrectly describe observations of the claimant. Medical records can contain factual errors. Handwritten records are sometimes difficult to read, leading to mistaken assumptions.

Finally, when a third party has limited information, that individual may provide inaccurate information. Context can profoundly influence behavior. If the source interacts with the claimant in a single context, erroneous conclusions can be drawn when the source attempts to generalize from the observed behavior to a wider range of contexts. Treatment providers, for example, often base their understanding of their patients on how their patients behave during appointments. Similarly, family members may never have observed the claimant in a work setting. A broad sampling of behavior is necessary in order to generalize about the claimant's behavior under other circumstances.

6
chapter

Psychological and Neuropsychological Test Data

Data from psychological and neuropsychological testing can provide very useful information in a disability evaluation. Some evaluators, however, tend to weight these data too heavily, without sufficient consideration to the limits of testing. Data obtained from psychological and neurological testing are especially vulnerable to methodological limitations. At the most basic level, the psychometric properties of the test (e.g., validity and reliability) must be adequate. The percentage of subjects correctly and incorrectly classified (sensitivity and specificity) is important. The evaluator must consider the rate of false positives and false negatives before reaching conclusions. The tests selected must be appropriate to the referral questions, administered in accordance with standard procedures, and valid for the purposes for which they are being used.

Even sound methodology can be quickly undermined when errors are made in the collection or interpretation of data. The evaluator should examine test data carefully to ensure that errors are not overlooked. Mistakes in test administration, scoring, and interpretation are easy to make. Test protocols should be reviewed for incorrect scoring of individual items and inaccuracies in calculating total scores. Great care should be taken when charts or tables are used to convert raw scores to standard scores or percentiles. In addition, the evaluator's degree of experience or skill with a particular test can have a profound effect on the accuracy of administration, scoring, and interpretation.

Test-interpretation strategies, including the decision to use computer-generated interpretations, affect the value of the data generated. Evaluators should remember that interpretive statements found in computer-generated reports are hypotheses to be verified and are not firm conclusions. The inferences derived from test results must not exceed the limits of the test itself. Since it is virtually impossible for a disability evaluator to directly test all the functional abilities

BEST PRACTICE

When analyzing psychometric data:

- Assess the psychometric properties of the test, including validity, reliability, sensitivity, and specificity.

- Carefully review test protocols and scoring summaries to check for errors.

- Understand the type of data each test yields and the nature of the hypotheses that can reasonably be generated from these data.

- Consider how closely the constructs assessed relate to the psycho-legal questions of the evaluation.

necessary for the performance of the claimant's job, a certain degree of extrapolation is required. Care must be taken not to wander too far from the constructs of the test. The more closely the test constructs relate to key functional abilities, the more useful the test data will be.

Step Four: Formulate Opinions

The final step in data interpretation is the formulation of the evaluator's opinions. This requires applying the findings of the evaluation to test the evaluator's hypotheses. As discussed earlier in this chapter, it should be expected that some of the data obtained in the course of the evaluation will be conflicting. Such inconsistencies should not be ignored or discarded, but should be incorporated into the process of hypothesis testing. This was described by Witt and Weitz (2007), who noted, "(A)n evaluation involves testing alternative hypotheses, perhaps none of which provides a perfect fit with the data. If more than one hypothesis is plausible, the evaluator is best served by considering the evidence for each and indicating how the evidence best supports one or the other" (p. 22). Using the evaluation data that have been organized and weighed (as described in the two preceding sections of this chapter), the evaluator should proceed in a systematic fashion to test the previously identified hypotheses.

Establishing the Presence of a Condition

As described earlier, a finding of "disability" requires that the claimant have an illness or injury that compromises his ability to work. Thus, the first issue to be considered is whether an illness or injury (i.e., a clinical condition) is present. The alternative hypotheses can be defined as follows:

- The claimant does not have a genuine clinical condition.
- The claimant does have a genuine clinical condition.

In order to test these hypotheses, the evaluator should consider evidence of signs and symptoms related to the claimant's alleged condition. The pattern of symptoms should be evaluated to determine if this pattern is consistent with patterns associated with known illnesses or injuries. The course of the claimant's condition can be compared with the expected progression of the alleged condition. Whether the claimant's response to treatment is credible should be gauged. In some cases, the evaluator may be asked to determine the claimant's diagnosis. If so, the evaluator should compare the claimant's symptoms and related features to standard diagnostic criteria. With the exception of Social Security disability, the precise diagnosis is less important than documenting that valid symptoms exist. The fact that the claimant's symptoms do not correspond completely with established diagnostic descriptions does not mean that a genuine clinical condition is not present.

Establishing the Existence of Functional Impairments

Functional impairments are the cornerstone of disability. The existence of a condition alone is not sufficient for a finding of disability. Impairments in functioning must be present as well. The alternative hypotheses to consider are:

- The claimant has no functional impairments.
- The claimant has functional impairments.

It is important for the evaluator to understand that disability involves a change in functional capacity. Functional impairments must be the product of an illness or injury. If the claimant manifests inadequate functioning due to other circumstances, the functional impairments would not be viewed as arising from an illness or injury, and would generally not constitute grounds for an occupational disability claim. Therefore, the evaluator must determine if the claimant's current functioning is worse than it was prior to the onset of the episode of illness or the injury, resulting in impairment relative to his or her baseline functioning.

The evaluator then needs to ascertain the nature of the claimant's functional impairments and the evidence in support of them. These functional impairments should be plausible given the type and severity of the claimant's condition. Genuine functional impairments are usually evident across the various aspects of the claimant's life. For example, in a claimant with bipolar disorder, it would be difficult to understand why the claimant's ability to maintain a stable mood would be impaired only in a work setting and not in a social venue.

Relating Functional Impairments to the Demands of the Claimant's Job

The nexus between functional impairments and work demands is at the core of disability evaluation. The presence of functional impairments does not in itself constitute the basis for a valid disability claim, unless these impairments also compromise the claimant's ability to work. Consider these alternative hypotheses:

- The claimant's functional impairments do not interfere with work capacity.
- The claimant's functional impairments interfere with work capacity.

In order to test these hypotheses, the evaluator must know the specific functional abilities necessary for the performance of the claimant's job. The evaluator should determine whether each functional ability is impaired. Given the functional abilities that are impaired, the evaluator must then judge whether the claimant can still perform the substantial and material duties of her occupation. The evaluator should also consider whether the claimant could perform her job if accommodations were made in the form of reduced hours or a decreased workload.

Ruling Out Other Causes of Work Impairment

The evaluator next must weigh the impact of other factors that may be affecting the claimant's ability to work. The existence of such factors does not necessarily mean that the claimant does not also have a genuine clinical condition and associated functional impairment. The alternative hypotheses are:

- The claimant is unable to work for reasons unrelated to a genuine clinical condition.
- The claimant is unable to work as a result of the functional impairments resulting from a genuine clinical condition.

As noted earlier, in order to have a valid disability claim, the claimant's current functioning must be worse than his baseline functioning, and this difference in functioning must be attributable to the effects of an illness or injury. In order to rule out work impairment resulting from other causes, the evaluator must consider whether other factors are present that would interfere with the claimant's ability to work. These factors might include legal issues (e.g., loss of professional license, incarceration); financial issues (e.g., decrease in work opportunities, rising costs of doing business); age (e.g., desire to retire); career issues (e.g., career dissatisfaction, unsuitability for chosen profession); personal issues (e.g., divorce and remarriage leading to a need to relocate, serious illness of a family member); negative publicity (e.g., arrest for drunk driving, malpractice case); and poor job performance (e.g., lack of skill or aptitude). If such factors are present, the evaluator needs to consider whether the claimant would be able to work if obstacles related to these factors were removed. If the claimant would still be unable to perform her job duties even with these obstacles removed, the evaluator would conclude that the inability to work is related to the claimant's condition and not these extraneous circumstances.

Conclusion

Data interpretation and analysis allow the evaluator to process and organize the data obtained in the course of the evaluation in order to formulate opinions. First the evaluator must identify relevant hypotheses. Next, the evaluator should organize the data to facilitate analysis. This can be accomplished along dimensions of timeframe, data source, and functional ability. The next step is to assess the data. It is likely that some of the data collected in the evaluation will be conflicting. The evaluator must be prepared to deal with these inconsistencies by assessing the validity and relevance of each piece of data. All data sources have inherent strengths and limitations. The evaluator can utilize this knowledge to assess the relative value of the data and its appropriateness in addressing specific issues.

The final step in the process of data analysis and interpretation involves systematically testing alternative hypotheses to determine which hypotheses best fit the data. Hypotheses should address the existence of a condition, the existence of functional impairments, how functional impairments relate to job duties, and whether factors other than the claimant's condition interfere with work functioning. In addition to describing the data supporting his or her opinions, the evaluator should cite the data not supporting the endorsed hypotheses, and be prepared to explain why the data supporting the alternative hypothesis is stronger.

Report Writing and Testimony | 7

Disability evaluations, almost without exception, require the creation of a written report. Unlike some types of civil litigation in which the evaluator presents his or her findings to the referral source to determine if a written report will be requested, in a disability evaluation, the evaluator should proceed immediately from collecting and interpreting the evaluation data to organizing and describing his findings in a report, which is then sent to the referral source. This chapter will describe how to organize a report, what information should (and should not) be included, the required level of detail, and the effective response to referral questions. It will also discuss the accurate communication of information. Finally, this chapter will describe how the written report can form the basis for testimony in court or in an administrative hearing.

Purpose of the Report

Evaluations are requested in disability cases to assist in the adjudication of the claim when the claims adjudicator lacks sufficient information about the claimant's condition and the associated functional limitations to determine if the claimant qualifies for disability benefits. Accordingly, the purpose of the disability evaluation is to provide information about the claimant's condition and the nature and extent of any related functional impairments. The written report should reflect this purpose. Thus, the evaluator should consider the type of information that is likely to be helpful to the claims adjudicator, and how this information can be communicated most effectively. It is important to emphasize that the

INFO
The purpose of the written report is to provide information that will be helpful to the claims adjudicator in determining whether the claimant is entitled to receive benefits.

evaluator is not being asked to render a decision as to whether the claimant is entitled to receive disability benefits. The report should focus on communicating information relevant to the questions presented in the referral.

Organizational Structure

Even good data collected in an evaluation are not useful unless they are organized in a manner allowing efficient and accurate communication to the referral source. Heilbrun (2001) stressed the importance of effectively organizing the forensic report, noting that, in most cases, the report is the final "product" of the forensic evaluation, and it must make clear what was done, for what purpose, and leading to what conclusions. This communication is facilitated by a report presented in sections. The Specialty Guidelines for Forensic Psychologists (1991) state, "Forensic psychologists make reasonable efforts to ensure that the products of their services . . . are communicated in ways that will promote understanding and avoid deception, given the particular characteristics, roles, and abilities of various recipients of the communications" (p. 663). The use of sections assists the reader in making sense of the information and creates a logical path from the presentation of the data collected to the formulation of the evaluator's opinion. This structure can also help the evaluator organize the data and explain it within the framework of the model selected for data interpretation. It also provides a clear separation of data and opinion.

There is no widely accepted format for a disability-evaluation report. Therefore, the evaluator is free to design whatever structure best facilitates the presentation of the relevant material. The following is an example of a format that organizes the material in a way that reflects the logical and chronological progression of the evaluation process, incorporating the critical information that should be communicated to the referral source. The sections in this suggested format include the Introduction, Procedures, Record Review, Behavioral Observations and Mental Status Data, Clinical Interview, Test Data, Collateral Contacts,

BEST PRACTICE
Organize your report into sections creating a logical path from presentation of data collected to the formulation of your opinion.

Formulation, and Answers to Referral Questions. Each will be discussed in the sections that follow.

Introduction

The report should begin with a section that summarizes key information that identifies the claimant and the context of the evaluation, and documents that informed consent was obtained. The claimant's full name and any identifying information related to the disability claim (e.g., claim number) should be included. It is helpful to note relevant dates, such as the claimant's date of birth, the date the claimed disability began, and the date(s) of the evaluation, at the top of the report. The evaluator's name and credentials should be clearly identified.

The context of the evaluation should be described, including identification of the referral source, the circumstances leading to the referral, and the claimant's current status with regard to the disability process (e.g., new request for benefits, reevaluation of ongoing claim, or disputed termination of benefits). If the matter is in the process of litigation, this should be noted. A statement regarding informed consent should be included in the introduction. This statement should indicate that the following information was disclosed to the claimant: (a) the identification of the party requesting the evaluation, (b) the reason for the evaluation, (c) that the purpose would be evaluation rather than treatment, (d) a written report would be created and sent to the referral source, (e) no feedback would be given to the claimant, and (f) any information shared or obtained in the course of the evaluation would be disclosed to the referral source. The manner in which this information was communicated to the claimant (i.e., orally, in writing, or both) should be described. It should be documented

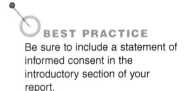

BEST PRACTICE
Be sure to include a statement of informed consent in the introductory section of your report.

that the claimant understood and agreed to the conditions of the evaluation and consented to proceed.

Procedures

In the next section, the procedures utilized in the evaluation should be described. The evaluator should list all the materials that he reviewed, such as medical and psychological treatment records, documents related to the disability claim, investigative reports, reports from previous evaluations, and financial or employment data. If collateral interviews were performed, the names of the sources, the dates and times of the interviews, and the nature of the contact (i.e., telephone or in person) must be included. The evaluator should list the dates and times the claimant was seen for the evaluation, delineating the time devoted to the interview and for psychological testing. A full list of all psychological and neuropsychological tests should be included. It is important to identify all instruments by full name and edition, not just by acronyms (e.g., "Wechsler Adult Intelligence Scale—Fourth Edition" rather than "WAIS"). If someone other than the evaluator of record, such as a psychometrician or a trainee, performed any part of the evaluation, this should be disclosed, with a clear indication of the extent of this person's involvement.

Summary of Records Reviewed

The report should include a section describing the content of all the materials the evaluator reviewed. It is important to consider the level of detail needed in this section. The evaluator should seek a middle ground between a brief description and an exhaustive rendition of this material. In most cases the referral source has provided this material to the evaluator, and therefore has access to and familiarity with the content of these records. On the other hand, the evaluator needs to demonstrate that she has read, understood, organized, and integrated the data in a meaningful way that furthers the purpose of the evaluation. In general, the record review should be sufficiently comprehensive so that if a record or the information it provides is relied upon, the record is cited in sufficient detail so that its source and content are clear to the reader. This can usually be accomplished by providing a cogent summary of the evaluator's understanding of the material reviewed, focusing this summary on issues most relevant to the referral questions. Although sometimes it may be useful to include direct quotes from the records, the review should not consist solely of lengthy verbatim excerpts. In addition, it is important to attribute data to the source from which they were obtained. For example, it is not enough to state, "The claimant has been diagnosed with bipolar disorder," but rather, "In 1998, the claimant's psychiatrist, Dr. Jones, diagnosed her with bipolar disorder." When records contain contradictory or ambiguous data, this should be noted. For example, "Dr. Smith's records indicate the claimant's diagnosis was 'Adjustment Disorder with depressed mood,' while Dr. Roberts reported a diagnosis of 'Major Depressive Disorder with psychotic features.'"

Behavioral Observations and Mental Status Data

It is very important to record the evaluator's observations of the claimant. This includes a basic physical description of the claimant, including grooming, clothing, and overall appearance. It should be noted whether the claimant arrived on time for the evaluation, the method of transportation utilized, and whether the claimant was accompanied by anyone. Observations regarding the claimant's attitude, affect, mood, eye contact, activity level, behavior, thought processes, attention span, speech, and language should be recorded. It is also important to document if there were any variations in these areas observed over the course of the evaluation.

Clinical Interview

The report should include a detailed account of the face-to-face interview with the claimant. It is helpful to begin with basic orienting information, such as the date, time, and duration of the interview. Beyond this, the bulk of this section of the report should be a systematic presentation of the information as reported by the claimant, organized in a manner that facilitates comprehension. As with the record review, the selective use of direct quotations can be an effective way to communicate these data. It is important to include detailed information about the claimant's history and current functioning, as described by the claimant. This should include personal history, such as where and by whom the claimant was raised, medical history, psychiatric history, and legal history. Particularly important is information about the claimant's educational history and occupational history. This will help establish an understanding of the claimant's current situation in relation to his baseline functioning.

The reported history of the claimant's disability should be described in detail. Was the onset gradual or sudden? When did the claimant's work functioning start to be affected? Did other people notice? At what point did she decide to file a claim for disability benefits? At what point did she seek treatment and from whom? Does the claimant plan to return to work, or is the disability viewed as permanent?

In addition to the preceding, it is also helpful to include the evaluator's observations regarding the manner in which the claimant communicated this information. Was the claimant easy to engage and eager to discuss his situation, or was the claimant reluctant to reveal information? Did he have difficulty recalling specific details or become upset when discussing certain material? Were there inconsistencies noted in the information provided by the claimant? If so, what attempts were made to clarify this information?

Test Data

When psychological or neuropsychological testing is used in a disability evaluation, a section of the report should be devoted to describing the findings. It is particularly important to communicate test data in a manner that will be easily understood and not misconstrued by the reader. Test data, more than information in the other sections of the report, employ a language that is "foreign" to the lay reader. Care must be taken to explain the findings using comprehensible language and to ensure that the evaluator does not overstate the significance of these data. Lay readers may incorrectly assume that, like X-rays and blood tests, psychological testing yields definitive conclusions. The evaluator should describe test data in a manner that leads to accurate assumptions and interpretations.

BEST PRACTICE
If you used psychological or neuropsychological testing in the evaluation, document your methods and findings in a separate section of the report, using laymen's terms.

To facilitate comprehension, test data can be grouped into logical categories. For example, the evaluator may have subsections for intellectual functioning, emotional functioning, and validity measures. She should begin each subsection with a brief description of the type of information she will present. Terms that will be used to describe the test data, such as *impaired* or *borderline*, should be operationally defined. The evaluator should identify individual instruments by name and with a description of what each instrument measures. It is helpful to include actual test scores, either within the text or in a separate addendum to the report. Although this information will not add much to a lay person's understanding, it will be useful when the report is reviewed by another professional.

Collateral Contacts

Information obtained from interviews with collateral sources should be discussed in a separate section of the report. Each source should be identified by name and by relationship to the claimant. The duration and nature of the contact (in person, by telephone) should be described. The evaluator should be sure to document that informed assent was obtained from the person who was interviewed. As with other sections of the report, the judicious use of direct quotations can be helpful in conveying collateral information. If unsuccessful attempts were made to obtain information from sources, this should also be noted.

Formulation

The formulation presents the evaluator's opinion as it was developed through considering and analyzing all the information collected over the course of the evaluation. Using the data of the

7
chapter

evaluation, the evaluator should clearly explain his opinion and the reasoning behind it. The formulation is not the place to present new information. Everything needed to understand the formulation should have already been presented in the body of the report. On the other hand, the formulation should not be a simple rehashing and restatement of the evaluation data. Instead, it is an opportunity to distill the data into a concise and comprehensible summation that follows logically from the data.

The formulation should be confined to information that is relevant to the purpose of the evaluation as defined by the referral questions. Evaluators should not offer opinions that go beyond the scope of their evaluation or the scope of their expertise. For example, a psychologist who was asked to evaluate the claimant's emotional functioning should not offer opinions about the claimant's neurocognitive status unless the evaluation yielded data relevant to this question. Nor should a psychologist exceed the scope of her professional license by offering her opinion about how a claimant's medical or physical condition affects his occupational functioning.

If requested, the evaluator should include a DSM diagnosis in the formulation. Again, this diagnosis should be consistent with and follow from the data that were collected during the evaluation. There should be a logical explanation of how diagnostic impressions were reached and a discussion of the data supporting these conclusions. It may be helpful for the evaluator to list the DSM diagnostic criteria for the disorder in question and then describe the evidence supporting the presence or absence of each element. The evaluator should avoid including diagnoses not addressed in the actual evaluation. For example, if the evaluator was asked to assess emotional functioning in a claimant with a history of a concussion, diagnoses regarding possible cognitive deficits should not be included unless the evaluation specifically assessed cognitive functioning. If, however, there is documented evidence of the presence of additional diagnoses, beyond what was specifically addressed in the evaluation, these diagnoses can be mentioned, but it should be clear that the

BEST PRACTICE
The formulation should be supported by the data presented in the body of the report. Do not introduce new material in this section.

current evaluation did not address those issues. In general, including "rule-out" diagnoses or diagnoses "by history," especially when the source of the history is limited to the claimant's self-report, should be avoided.

Opinions on Referral Questions

Most referrals for disability evaluations include a list of questions to be addressed by the evaluation. Each referral question should be clearly answered. To ensure this is accomplished, it is helpful to have a separate section of the report listing each question and the evaluator's response. As with the formulation, the basis for each answer should be contained within the body of the report. The response to each question should refer to the report data supporting the answer.

The evaluator must read each question carefully to confirm that his response is on point and encompasses all aspects of the question. It is important that the evaluator address every aspect of each question and not offer opinions beyond the referral questions. For example, the response to a question regarding the presence of a specific diagnosis should not include references to other diagnoses. On the other hand, the evaluator's response to a question asking about a specific diagnosis or any other diagnoses should include both whether the specific diagnosis is present and whether or not additional diagnoses are present.

There may be times when the evaluator is unable to answer one or more of the referral questions. This may be due to lack of cooperation on the claimant's part, the unavailability of certain records or collateral sources, or the nature of the question itself, given the tools available to the evaluator. For example, the evaluator may not be able to answer a question about how the claimant will behave in the future (e.g., "What will the claimant's condition be two years from now?"). Likewise, the evaluator will not be able to address questions outside of her expertise (e.g., "If the claimant is not depressed, does his heart condition alone impair his ability to work?"). Non-physicians (unless they possess specific training in this area) should generally avoid answering specific questions about medication doses and other aspects of pharmacological treatment.

7
chapter

It is acceptable to answer such questions in a general way (e.g., "Cognitive behavioral therapy in combination with antidepressant medication is generally considered an effective treatment for depression"), but specific answers, such as "The claimant should be on an SSRI," should be avoided. The best way to handle unanswerable questions is to explain why the question cannot be answered and, when possible, explain what could be done to obtain the necessary information (e.g., a collateral interview with the claimant's psychiatrist; obtaining treatment records from claimant's recent hospitalization). Ideally, this information should be communicated to the referral source prior to completing the report so that the necessary information can be obtained, if possible.

Use of Language in Reports

The first part of this chapter focused on what to include in the evaluation report. This section will focus on how to communicate this information most effectively. Certain words or phrases may have unintended connotations, given the differing backgrounds and experiences of the writer and the reader. Terms such as "disability" have a legally defined meaning in the context of a disability claim. Other terms, such as "depression," are frequently used in general conversation but may not refer to the specific diagnostic entity described in the DSM.

When referring to the person being evaluated, it is preferable to use terms such as "claimant," "insured," or "examinee." The subject of the evaluation should never be referred to as the "patient" or "client." Such terms reflect a treatment relationship rather than evaluative relationship. The term "plaintiff" should be used only if the evaluation is being conducted during actual litigation and only if the examinee is in fact the plaintiff in this matter. (Claimants are sometimes sued by the insurance company, in which case the claimant is the defendant rather than the plaintiff.) "Claimant" is a neutral term and is appropriate in all circumstances. If the claimant is referred to by name, the claimant's last name and title should be used. This reflects respect for the claimant as well as the formal, non-therapeutic nature of the evaluation. The use of first names in an evaluation of this type is inappropriate. The use of surnames and titles extends to all people over the age of majority who are referred to in the report, including family members, therapists, and attorneys. Professionals, such as doctors and lawyers, should be referred to by their appropriate title (e.g., "Dr. Jones" rather than "Ms. Jones").

BEWARE
It is inappropriate in the written report to refer to the claimant by first name. Last name and title should always be used to reflect the formal nature of the evaluation.

As with all assessments, it is important to avoid the use of language that conveys any type of bias. All parties discussed in the report should be described in language that minimizes such bias as much as possible. Regardless of the evaluator's opinion, neither the claimant nor any party mentioned should be described in a pejorative manner. This is particularly important if the evaluator is making an assertion that the claimant may be malingering, or when the claimant has engaged in behavior that is distasteful to the evaluator (e.g., sexual improprieties with children). Regardless of the evaluator's feelings about the claimant, neutral, professional language should be utilized in the report. Terminology that conveys any sense of prejudice against the claimant based on age, sex, religion, race, or ethnicity is completely inappropriate.

It is very important to avoid the use of jargon and undefined technical terms. The evaluator must not assume that readers all know what bipolar disorder is, or that the concept of a T-score is common knowledge. Unfamiliar terms must be defined so that the reader will understand the meaning of the report without having to use a medical dictionary. Language used to describe mental status is often meaningless to lay readers. For example, the meaning of "oriented times four," "blunted affect," "euthymic mood," or "circumstantial speech" may be lost on the average person. Likewise, diagnostic labels are often poorly understood. Some people confuse "schizophrenia" with "dissociative disorder" or assume that major depression is synonymous with "feeling blue." The terms "neuropsychological" and "neurological" are often confused. In addition, lay readers are often unclear about the difference between psychiatrist, psychologist, and psychotherapist, and use these terms interchangeably.

Psychological testing is perhaps the area that is most difficult for the evaluator to convey in a meaningful way to a lay reader. Many terms frequently used to present psychological testing results are not typically understood by lay readers, including "standard deviation," "confidence interval," "T-score," and "index score." The evaluator should describe what each instrument is measuring and what the scores mean. In other words, does a score of 80 mean the examinee got 80% of the items right, does it mean he or she performed better than 80% of similar people who have taken the test, or does it mean he or she performed in the "low average" range?

The evaluator then needs to describe how the examinee performed on the testing and the types of inferences that can be derived from this performance. For example, it must be clear that having an elevation on Scale 4 of the MMPI-2 does not "prove" the claimant is a psychopathic deviant; nor does performing poorly on the TOMM "prove" that the claimant is able to return to work. Test results should be described in accessible terms and plain language.

Finally, the one word that should not be used to convey the evaluator's opinion in a disability evaluation is "disability." As has been discussed throughout this volume, *disability* is a legally defined term that is beyond the ken of the evaluator to determine. The use of this term has a specific meaning and connotation in a disability evaluation that is not synonymous with other uses of this word. Thus, while there is no problem with using the word "disability" when quoting someone else (e.g., "the claimant stated he has been disabled since the accident"), the evaluator should not otherwise use this word (e.g., "the claimant was disabled by the accident").

BEST PRACTICE
Keep your reports jargon-free. If it is necessary to include clinical or technical terms, be sure to clarify their meaning and relevance.

BEWARE
Avoid using the word "disability" in conveying your opinion. Frame your discussion in terms of functional impairments and work capacity.

Dealing with Ultimate Issue Questions

Ideally, the evaluator should not be asked to determine disability. Rather, the evaluator should be asked to describe the claimant's condition, functional capacity, and impairments. For the reasons previously described, the evaluator is not in a position to answer the "ultimate issue question," as he lacks important information necessary to make this determination. Sometimes, however, the evaluator will be asked this question, or he may assume that he is being asked to determine disability. In such circumstances, an important concept to remember is that "inability to work" is not the same as "disability." The evaluator may have and express an opinion regarding the claimant's ability to return to work. Questions about work ability ask the evaluator to consider the nature of the claimant's condition and her impairments relative to the demands and requirements of her job rather than to make a legal determination of "disability" status or eligibility for disability benefits. Stating that the claimant is not able to return to work is not the same as stating that the claimant is disabled. Keeping this distinction in mind allows the evaluator to respond to questions related to work capacity without making ultimate-issue statements. The evaluator may be asked directly, "Is the claimant disabled?" If so, her answer can be couched in terms of the claimant's "ability to work." For example, the evaluator could respond to this question by stating, "The claimant demonstrated significant impairments in memory that would most likely prevent her from being able to work as an accountant," or "No significant impairments in cognitive or emotional functioning were identified in this evaluation that would prevent the claimant from being able to work as a trial lawyer."

Requests for Changes

Occasionally, after the report has been completed and delivered to the referral source, the evaluator may be contacted and asked to make changes to the report. There are a number of reasons for this, and it is important that the evaluator understand the reason for the request before deciding how to respond.

7
chapter

The most frequent reason that referral sources request report changes is to correct typographical errors. Careful proofreading should be completed before delivering the report. It is not sufficient to "spell-check" a document. Proofreading is especially important when reports are dictated by the evaluator and typed by someone else. Dates, names, and test scores should be carefully checked. Another common error is the omission of a critical word in a sentence (omitting the word "not," for example). Although seemingly minor, typographical errors do not reflect well on the evaluator, who may be seen as being inattentive to details or careless. Such errors also raise questions about the accuracy of other information (e.g., test scores) reported by the evaluator and may diminish the referral source's confidence in the overall evaluation. When confronted with a request to correct such errors, the evaluator should do so immediately, without making any other alterations to the report.

Another situation in which changes may be requested is when the evaluator has inadvertently misrepresented, misunderstood, or overlooked some factual data. Examples of these errors include such things as the evaluator referring to the disability claim as originating in 2006 rather than 1996; the claimant's job being described as "a physician" rather than "a physician's assistant," or the evaluator stating there were no treatment records for the previous year when, in fact, there were. These errors are serious, as incorrect assumptions such as these can change the evaluator's understanding of the claimant's situation and his opinion regarding the claimant's functional capacity. If the referral source identifies factual errors, the evaluator will be contacted and provided with accurate information. The evaluator should then reconsider his opinion in light of this in order to determine if this corrected information changes his conclusions. Even if the evaluator's opinion remains unchanged, it is necessary for him to formally respond to the referral source, acknowledge that he understands of the corrected information, and state whether or not this information changes his opinion. This document becomes an addendum to the evaluator's report.

Sometimes the referral source will obtain information that was not available at the outset of the evaluation, such as updated treatment records or surveillance reports. If provided with additional data, the evaluator should review these data and, as above, generate an addendum to the report, including a review of the additional material, and the extent to which (if at all) this new information alters the evaluator's previously expressed opinions.

In some circumstances, the referral source may not fully understand the evaluator's opinion. This may be due to the use of technical language or the way in which the evaluator stated her opinion. This also occurs when the evaluator equivocates and does not fully answer a referral question. Regardless of whether the evaluator believes she has been clear, if the referral source does not understand something, it needs to be clarified. The evaluator should prepare an addendum to the report providing an additional explanation of the statements in question.

Except in the circumstances just described, the evaluator should never amend her opinion once the report has been completed. The report itself should never be altered except to correct minor typographical errors. For changes to the content of the report that go beyond this, the evaluator must create an addendum to the original report as a separate document.

Sometimes the evaluator will receive a request (or even a subpoena) for the release of his report, test data, or notes from the claimant, her lawyer, attending physician, or another insurance company. In such circumstances, the appropriate response is to notify the referral source (i.e., the evaluator's "client"). Ideally, the request will be handled directly by the company. If the claim has progressed to litigation, contacting the legal department of the referring insurance company is the best place to begin. Under no circumstances should the evaluator release any material or discuss

7
chapter

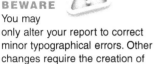

BEWARE
You may
only alter your report to correct
minor typographical errors. Other
changes require the creation of
an addendum to the original
report.

his findings with any party other than the referral source without authorization.

From Written Report to Testimony

Relatively few disability cases require testimony in court. However, when the evaluator is required to testify in court or at an administrative hearing, a well-crafted written report can provide an effective outline for her testimony. As described by Heilbrun (2001), testimony is based on the data obtained in the course of the evaluation. If the data collected are insufficient to support the evaluator's conclusions, this cannot lead to effective testimony. Ethical standards also address this issue. The American Psychological Association (APA) Code of Ethics (2002)states: "Psychologists' work is based upon established scientific and professional knowledge of the discipline" (Section 2.04[a]). It also notes: "Psychologists base the opinions contained in their recommendations, reports, and diagnostic or evaluative statements, including forensic testimony, on information and techniques sufficient to substantiate their findings" (Section 9.01). Conceptualized in this way, it becomes clear that a properly designed and conducted evaluation provides the foundation for a cogent written report, which in turn provides the foundation for effective expert testimony.

Admissibility of scientific expert testimony is determined by applicable evidentiary standards. Under the *Frye* (1923) standard, to be admissible, expert testimony must be based on data and techniques that have gained "general acceptance" in the expert's field. The *Daubert* (1993) standard mirrors the Federal Rules of Evidence. Under this standard, admissibility decisions may incorporate several factors, including the relevance of the underlying technique or theory to the specific facts of the case, whether the underlying technique or theory is testable and falsifiable, whether it has been peer-reviewed and has been generally accepted in the field, and

BEST PRACTICE
Let your written report serve as an outline for your testimony.

whether there is a known error rate. These factors should be considered when the evaluator is planning and conducting the evaluation to ensure that the methods utilized will ultimately meet legal admissibility standards.

Effective testimony requires clear and persuasive communication. As with the written report, it is critical to employ everyday language to explain the findings and conclusions of one's evaluation. As noted in the Specialty Guidelines for Forensic Psychologists (1991) IV A (2): "A full explanation of the results of tests and the bases for conclusions should be given in language that the client can understand." Evaluators have "an obligation to all parties to a legal proceeding to present their findings, conclusions, evidence, or other professional products in a fair manner," but they should also be prepared to deliver a "forceful representation of the data and reasoning upon which a conclusion or professional product is based" (SGFP, 1991, IV[D]). In doing so, evaluators must be careful to not misrepresent the weight, nature, or certainty of the evaluation findings and must not allow any other party to do so. As stated in the APA Ethics Code, "Psychologists do not knowingly make public statements that are false, deceptive, or fraudulent concerning their research, practice, or other work activities" (Section 5.01 [a]); and "If psychologists learn of misuse or misrepresentation of their work, they take reasonable steps to correct or minimize the misuse or misrepresentation" (Section 1.01).

Conclusion

Upon completion of data collection and analysis, the disability evaluator should prepare a written report to be delivered to the referral source. This report is the primary product of the evaluation and must encapsulate the evaluator's findings and opinions. The report should reflect the purpose of the disability evaluation, which is to provide data about the claimant's condition and the nature and extent of any related functional impairments.

There is no standard format for a disability evaluation report, but some type of organizational structure should be employed in order to efficiently and accurately communicate the evaluation

7 chapter

findings to the referral source. The use of sections in a report facilitates this communication. A logical organizational structure also assists the evaluator in organizing and explaining the data and provides a clear separation of data and opinion.

Disability evaluations typically begin with an introduction and contain sections describing the procedures, record review, behavioral observations, clinical interview, test data, collateral data, formulation, and responses to referral questions. Throughout the report, it is essential that the evaluator use accurate and comprehensible language to describe the evaluation. The use of professional jargon and undefined technical terms should be avoided, as these can result in the evaluator's findings' being misunderstood.

The evaluator should remain cognizant of the problems involved in making "ultimate issue statements," which, in the case of these evaluations, concern the determination of the claimant's disability status. The evaluator should remain focused on describing claimant's condition, functional capacity, and impairments. Although disability evaluations can include a discussion of the claimant's "ability to work," a determination of disability can only be made by a party familiar with the relevant legal standards.

Although most disability evaluations will not lead to litigation, when the evaluator is required to testify, the written report can provide a basis and an outline for the testimony. As with the written report, the evaluator must communicate his findings clearly, using everyday language. The evaluator must take care not to misrepresent or allow anyone else to misrepresent the nature or strength of his findings. This, however, does not preclude the evaluator from testifying in a manner that is strong and persuasive.

References

Abraham, K. (2000). *A concise restatement of torts*. St. Paul, MN: American Law Institute Publishers.

Adler, D., et al. (2006). Job performance deficits due to depression. *American Journal of Psychiatry, 163*(9), 1569–1576.

Alwes, Y. R., Clark, J. A., Berry, D. T. R., & Granacher, R. P. (2008). Screening for feigning in a civil forensic setting. *Journal of Clinical and Experimental Neuropsychology, 30*(2), 1–8.

American Medical Association (2008). *Guidelines to the evaluation of permanent impairment*, sixth Ed. Chicago, IL: American Medical Association Press.

American Psychiatric Association (2000). *Diagnostic and statistical manual of mental disorders*, fourth Ed., text revision. Washington, DC: American Psychiatric Association.

American Psychological Association (2002). *American Psychological Association ethical principles of psychologists and code of conduct*. Retrieved January 24, 2010, from http://www.apa.org/ethics/code2002.html.

Arbisi, P. A., & Ben-Porath, Y. S. (1995). An MMPI-2 infrequent response scale for use with psychopathological populations: The infrequency psychopathology scale, F(p). *Psychological Assessment, 7*, 424–431.

Archer, R. P., Buffinton-Vollum, J. K., Stredney, R. V., & Handel, R. W. (2006). A survey of psychological test use patterns among forensic psychologists. *Journal of Personality Assessment, 87*(1), 84–94.

Autor, David H., and Duggan, M. G. (2006). The growth in the Social Security disability rolls: A fiscal crisis unfolding. *Journal of Economic Perspectives, 20*(3), 71–96.

Bagby, M., Nicholson, R., Bacchiochi, J., Ryder, A., & Bury, A. (2002). The predictive capacity of the MMPI-2 and PAI validity scales and indexes to detect coached and uncoached feigning. *Journal of Personality Assessment, 78*(1) 69–86.

Barth, P. (1990). Workers compensation for mental stress. *Behavioral Sciences and the Law, 8*(4) 349–360.

Beck, A. T. (1987). *Beck depression inventory*. San Antonio, TX: The Psychological Corporation.

Beck, A. T., & Steer, R. A. (1990). *Beck anxiety inventory manual*. Toronto: Psychological Corporation.

Boccaccini, M. T., & Brodsky, S. L. (1999). Test use in emotional injury cases. *Professional Psychology: Research and Practice, 30*(3), 253–259.

Bohigian, G. M., et al. (1996). Substance abuse and dependence in physicians: The Missouri Physicians' Health Program. *Southern Medical Journal, 89*(11), 1078–1080.

Borkowska, A., & Rybakowski, J. A. (2001). Neuropsychological frontal lobe tests indicate that bipolar depressed patients are more impaired than unipolar. *Bipolar Disorders, 3*(1), 88– 94.

Brewin, C., Kleiner, J. S., & Vasterling, J. J. (2007). Memory for emotionally neutral information in posttraumatic stress disorder: A meta-analytic investigation. *Journal of Abnormal Psychology, 116*(3), 448–463.

Briere, J. (1995). *Trauma symptom inventory professional manual*. Odessa, FL: Psychological Assessment Resources.

Brunello, N., et al. (2001). Posttraumatic stress disorder: Diagnosis and epidemiology, comorbidity and social consequences, biology and treatment. *Neuropsychobiology, 43*, 150–162.

Burges, C., & McMillan, T. M. (2001). The ability of naive participants to report symptoms of post-traumatic stress disorder. *British Journal of Clinical Psychology, 40*, 209–214.

Butcher, J. N., Graham, J. R., Ben-Porath, Y. S., Tellegen, A., Dahlstrom, W. G., & Kaemmer, B. (2001). MMPI-2: Manual for administration and scoring (rev. ed.). Minneapolis, MN: University of Minnesota Press.

Cohen, Y., Lachenmeyer, J. R., & Springer, C. (2003). Anxiety and selective attention in obsessive-compulsive disorder. *Behavior Research and Therapy, 41*(11), 1311–1323.

Committee on Ethical Guidelines for Forensic Psychologists (1991). "Specialty guidelines for forensic psychologists," *Law and Human Behavior, 15*(6), 655–665.

Defense Research Institute (2006). *Insurance bad faith: A compendium of state law*. Chicago: DRI.

Derogatis, L. R. (1977). SCL-90-R, administration, scoring & procedures manual—I for the Revised version. Baltimore, MD: John Hopkins University School of Medicine.

Dewa, C., et al. (2003). Pattern of antidepressant use and duration of depression-related absence from work. *British Journal of Psychiatry, 183*, 507–513.

Drake, A., et al. (2000). Factors predicting return to work following mild traumatic brain injury: A discriminate analysis. *Journal of Head Trauma and Rehabilitation, 15*(5), 1103–1112.

Duka, T., et al. (2003). Impairment in cognitive functions after multiple detoxifications in alcoholic inpatients. *Alcoholism: Clinical and Experimental Research, 27*(10), 1563–1572.

Elahi, J., et al. (2004). Discriminating malingered from genuine civilian posttraumatic stress disorder: A validation of three MMPI-2 infrequency scales (F, Fp, and Fptsd). *Assessment, 11*(2), 139–144.

Estroff, S., Patrick, D., Zimmer, C., & Lachicotte, W. (1997). Pathways to disability income among persons with severe persistent psychiatric disorders. *Millbank Quarterly, 75*(4), 495–532.

Ettner, S., et al. (1997). The impact of psychiatric disorders on labor market outcome. *Industrial and Labor Relations Review, 51*(1) 64–81.

Farkas, M., Rosenfeld, B., Robbins, R., & van Gorp, W. (2006). Do tests of malingering concur? Concordance among malingering measures. *Behavioral Sciences and the Law, 24*(5), 659–71.

Fireman, B., et al. (2001). The prevalence of clinically recognized obsessive-compulsive disorder in a large health maintenance organization. *American Journal of Psychiatry, 158*(11), 1904–1910.

Flaro, L., Green, P., & Robertson, E. (2007). Word Memory Test failure 23 times higher in mild brain injury than in parents seeking custody: The power of external incentives. *Brain Injury, 21*(4) 373–383.

Fox, D., Lees-Haley, P., Earnest, K., & Dolezal-Wood, S. (1995). Base rates of post-concussive symptoms in health maintenance organization patients and controls. *Neuropsychology, 9*(4), 606–611.

Fraser, R., et al. (2006). Return to work in traumatic brain injury (TBI): A perspective on capacity for job complexity. *Journal of Vocational Rehabilitation, 25*, 141–148.

Frederick, R. I. (1997). *VIP (validity indicator profile) manual.* Minneapolis, MN: NCS Pearson.

Gallegos, K. V., et al. (1992). Relapse and recovery: Five- to ten-year follow-up study of chemically dependent physicians—The Georgia experience. *Maryland Medical Journal, 41*(4), 315– 319.

Gervais, R. (2005, April). Development of an empirically derived response bias scale for the MMPI-2. Paper presented at the Annual MMPI-2 Symposium and Workshops, Ft. Lauderdale, FL, USA.

Gervais, R., Ben-Porath, Y., Wygant, D., & Green, P. Development and validation of a response bias scale (RBS) for the MMPI-2. *Assessment, 14*(2), 196–208.

Glass, L. (Ed.) (2004). *Occupational medicine practice guidelines: Evaluation and management of common health problems and functional recovery of workers,* (2nd ed.). Elk Grove Village, IL: American College of Occupational and Environmental Medicine.

Gold, L. H., Anfang, S. A., Drukteinis, A. M., Metzner, J. L., Price, M., Wall, B. W., Wylonis, L., & Zonana, H. V. (2008). AAPL practice guideline for the forensic evaluation of psychiatric disability. *Journal of the American Academy of Psychiatry and the Law, 36*(4), (Suppl.), S3–S50.

Gold, L. H., & Shuman, D. W. (2009). *Evaluating mental health disability in the workplace.* New York: Springer.

Gold, M. S., et al. (2006). Fentanyl abuse and dependence: Further evidence for second hand exposure hypothesis. *Journal of Addictive Diseases, 25*(1), 15–21.

Goldberg, R., & Steury, S. (2001). Depression in the workplace: Costs and barriers to treatment. *Psychiatric Services, 53*(12) 1639–1643.

Green, B. (2003). Post-traumatic stress disorder: Symptom profiles in men and women. *Current Medical Research and Opinion, 19*(3), 200–204.

Green P. (2003). Manual for the *Word Memory Test for Windows.* Edmonton: Green's Publishing.

Greenberg, S., Otto, R., & Long, A. (2003). The utility of psychological testing in assessing emotional damages in personal injury litigation. *Assessment, 10*(4), 411–419.

Greenberg, S., & Shuman, D. (1997). Irreconcilable conflict between therapeutic and forensic roles. *Professional Psychology: Research & Practice, 28*(1), 50–57.

Greiffenstein, M. F., Baker, W. J., & Johnson-Greene, D. (2002). Actual versus self-reported scholastic achievement of litigating post-concussion and severe closed head injury claimants. *Psychological Assessment, 14*(2), 202–208.

Greisberg, S., & McKay, D. (2003). Neuropsychology of obsessive-compulsive disorder: A review and treatment implications. *Clinical Psychology Review, 23*(1), 95–117.

Grisso, T. (2003). *Evaluating competencies: Forensic assessments and instruments* (2nd ed.). New York: Kluwer Academic/Plenum Press.

Hall, R. C., & Chapman, M. J. (2005). Definition, diagnosis, and forensic implications of post-concussional syndrome. *Psychosomatics, 46*(3), 195–202.

Hammen, C., Gitlin, M., & Altshuler, L. (2000). Predictors of work adjustment in bipolar I patients: A naturalistic longitudinal follow-up. *Journal of Consulting and Clinical Psychology, 68*(2), 220–225.

Harper, C. (2007). The neurotoxicity of alcohol. *Human & Experimental Toxicology, 26*, 251– 257.

Hasin, D., et al. (2007). Prevalence, correlates, disability, and comorbidity of DSM-IV alcohol abuse and dependence in the United States. *Archives of General Psychiatry, 64*(7), 830– 842.

Hasin, D. S., et al. (2005). Epidemiology of major depressive disorder: Results from the National Epidemiological Survey on Alcoholism and Related Conditions. *Archives of General Psychiatry, 62*(10), 1097–1106.

Health Insurance Association of America (2000). *The source book of health insurance data, 1999–2000*. Washington, DC: HIAA.

Heilbrun, K. (1992). The role of psychological testing in forensic assessment. *Law and Human Behavior, 16*, 257–272.

Heilbrun, K. (2001). *Principles of forensic mental health assessment.* New York: Klewer.

Heilbrun, K., Grisso, T., & Goldstein, A. (2008). *Foundations of forensic mental health assessment.* New York: Oxford University Press.

Heilbrun, K., Rogers, R., & Otto, R. (2002). Forensic assessment: Current status and future directions. In J. Ogloff (Ed.), *Psychology and law: Reviewing the discipline* (pp. 120–147). New York: Kluwer Academic/Plenum Press.

Heilbrun, K., Warren, J., & Picarello, K. (2003). Third party information in forensic assessment. In I. B. Weiner (series ed.) & A. M. Goldstein (vol. ed.), *Handbook of Psychology: Vol. 11. Forensic psychology* (pp. 69–86). Hoboken, NJ: Wiley.

Heilbrun, K., Rosenfeld, B., Warren, J., & Collins, S. (1994). The use of third-party information in forensic assessments: A two-state comparison. *Bulletin of the American Academy of Psychiatry and the Law, 22*(3): 399–406.

Horwitz, J. E., & McCaffrey, R. J. (2006). A review of internet sites regarding independent medical examinations: Implications for clinical neuropsychological practitioners. *Applied Neuropsychology, 13*(3), 175–179.

Hurtz, G. M., & Donovan, J. J. (2000). Personality and job performance: The Big Five revisited. *Journal of Applied Psychology, 85,* 869–879.

Johnson, T., & Johnson, W. G. (2006). "The health care crisis for people with disabilities who do not receive social insurance benefits." Paper presented at the annual meeting of the Economics of Population Health: Inaugural Conference of the American Society of Health Economists, Madison, WI. Retrieved on 2008/10/09 from http://www.allacademic.com/meta/p93504_index.html.

Kane, A. (2008). Forensic psychology, psychological injuries, and the law. *Psychological Injury and Law, 1*(1), 36–58.

Kaye, S. (2004). *Fluctuating disability rates among working-age adults: Economic versus epidemiologic factors.* Paper presented at the American Public Health Association 132nd annual meeting and exposition, hosted by the American Public Health Association.

Kennedy, B. L., et al. (2002). Work, social, and family disabilities of subjects with anxiety and depression. *Southern Medical Journal, 95*(12), 1424–1427.

Kessler, R., et al. (1995). Posttraumatic stress disorder in the national comorbidity survey. *Archives of General Psychiatry, 52*(12), 1048–1060.

Kessler, R., Akiskal, H., Ames, M., et al. (2006). Prevalence and effects of mood disorders on work performance in a nationally representative sample of U.S. workers. *American Journal of Psychiatry, 163*(9), 1561–1568.

Kessler, R., et al. (1999). Depression in the workplace: Effects on short-term disability. *Health Affairs, 18*(5), 163–171.

Kessler, R., et al. (2008). Comparative and interactive effects of depression relative to other health problems on work performance in the workforce of a large employer. *Journal of Occupational and Environmental Medicine, 50*(7), 809–816.

Koch, W. J., O'Neill, M., & Douglas, K. (2005). Empirical limits for the forensic assessment of PTSD litigants. *Law and Human Behavior, 29*(1), 121–149).

Lally, S. (2003). What tests are acceptable for use in forensic evaluation? A survey of experts. *Professional Psychology: Research & Practice, 34*(5), 491–498.

Larrabee, G. (2007). *Assessment of malingered neuropsychological deficits.* New York: Oxford University Press.

Larrabee, G. (2008). Aggregation across multiple indicators improves the detection of malingering: relationship to likelihood ratios. *Clinical Neuropsychologist, 22*(8) 666–679.

Latas, M., et al. (2004). Predictors of work disabilities in patients with panic disorder with agoraphobia. European Psychiatry, 19(5) 280–284.

Lees-Haley, P. R., English, L. T., & Glenn, W. J. (1991). A fake bad scale on the MMPI-2 for personal injury claimants. *Psychological Reports, 68*, 208–210.

Lees-Haley, P. R., & Dunn, J. T. (1994). The ability of naive subjects to report symptoms of mild brain injury, PTSD, major depression and generalized anxiety disorder. *Journal of Clinical Psychology, 50*, 252–256.

Lees-Haley, P. R., Williams, C. W., Zasler, N. D., Marguilies, S., English, L. T., & Stevens, K. B. (1997). Response bias in plaintiffs' histories. *Brain Injury, 11*(11), 791–799.

Lehman, W., & Bennett, J. (2002). Job risk and employee substance use: The influence of personal background and work environment factors. *American Journal of Drug and Alcohol Abuse, 28*(2), 263–286.

Leo, R. J., & Del Regno, P. (2001). Social Security claims of psychiatric disability: Elements of case adjudication and the role of primary care physicians. *Primary Care Companion Journal of Clinical Psychiatry, 3*(6), 255–262.

Lewis, D., Rubin, P., & Drake, C. (2006). Expanding the net: Suggestions for forensic mental health examiners on identifying and obtaining third-party information. *Journal of Forensic Psychology Practice, 6*(2) 39–51.

Lynch, W. J. (2004). Determination of effort level, exaggeration, and malingering in neurocognitive assessment. *Journal of Head Trauma Rehabilitation, 19*(3) 277–283.

MacQueen, G., Parkin, C., Marriott, M., & Hasey, G. (2007). The long-term impact of treatment with electroconvulsive therapy on discrete memory systems in patients with bipolar disorder. *Journal of Psychiatry and Neuroscience, 32*(4), 241–249.

Malhi, G., Ivanovski, B., Hadzi-Pavlovic, D., Mitchell, P. B., Vieta, E., & Sachdev, P. (2007). Neuropsychological deficits and functional impairment in bipolar depression, hypomania and euthymia. *Bipolar Disorders, 9*(1–2), 114–125.

Marlowe, D. (1995). A hybrid decision framework for evaluating psychometric evidence. *Behavioral Sciences and the Law, 13*, 207–228.

Martinez-Aran, A., Vieta, E., Reinares, M., Colom, F. et al. (2004). Cognitive function across manic or hypermanic, depressed and euthymic states in bipolar disorder. *American Journal of Psychiatry, 161*(2), 262–270.

Martinez-Aran, A., Vieta, E., Reinares, M., et al. (2002). Neuropsychological performance in depressed and euthymic bipolar patients. *Neuropsychobiology, 46*(Suppl 1), 16–21.

Martinez-Aran, A., Vieta, E., Torrent, C., et al. (2007). Functional outcome in bipolar disorder: The role of clinical and cognitive factors. *Bipolar Disorders, 9*(1–2), 103–113.

Matthews, L. (2005). Work potential of road accident survivors with post-traumatic stress disorder. *Behaviour Research and Therapy, 43*(4), 475–483.

McCrimmon, S., & Oddy, M. (2006). Return to work following moderate-to-severe traumatic brain injury. *Brain Injury, 20*(10), 1037–1046.

Mechanic, D., et al. (2002). Employing persons with serious mental illness. *Health Affairs, 21*(5), 242–253.

Melton, G., Petrila, J., Poythress, N., & Slobogin, C. (2007). *Psychological evaluations for the court* (3rd ed.). New York: Guilford Publications.

Michalak, E., et al. (2007). The impact of bipolar disorder on work functioning: A qualitative analysis. *Bipolar Disorders, 9*, 126–143.

Miller, H. A. (2001). *M-FAST: Miller forensic assessment of symptoms test.* Lutz, FL: Psychological Assessment Resources.

Millward, L., et al. (2005). Depression and the perpetuation of an incapacitated identity as an inhibitor of return to work. *Journal of Psychiatric and Mental Health Nursing, 12*, 565– 573.

Millon, T., Davis, R., Millon, C., & Grossman, S. (2006). *Millon Clinical Multiaxial Inventory-III manual* (3rd ed.). Minneapolis, MN: National Computer Systems.

Mittenberg, W., et al. (2002). Base rates of malingering and symptom exaggeration. *Journal of Clinical and Experimental Neuropsychology, 24*(8) 1094–1102.

Morey, L. C. (1991). *Professional manual for the Personality Assessment Inventory.* Odessa, FL: Psychological Assessment Resources.

Morgan, V., et al. (2005). The epidemiology of bipolar disorder: Sociodemographic, disability and service utilization data from the Australian national study of low prevalence (psychotic) disorders. *Bipolar Disorders, 7*, 326–337.

Moore, B., & Donders, J. (2004). Predictors of invalid neuropsychological test performance after traumatic brain injury. *Brain Injury, 18*(10) 975–984.

Mullahy, J., & Sindelar, J. (1993). Alcoholism, work, and income. *Journal of Labor Economics, 11*(3), 493–520.

Murray, H. A. (1943). *Thematic apperception test manual.* Cambridge, MA: Harvard University Press.

National Institute of Mental Health (2001). *The numbers count: Mental disorders in America.* NIMH Publication No. 01–4584. Washington, DC.

Nelson, N., Sweet, J., & Dumakis, G. (2006). Meta-analysis of the MMPI-2 Fake Bad Scale: Utility in forensic practice. *Clinical Neuropsychologist, 20*(1), 39–58.

Nelson, N., Sweet, J., & Heilbronner, R. (2007). Examination of the new MMPI-2 Response Bias Scale (Gervais): Relationship with MMPI-2 validity scales. *Journal of Clinical and Experimental Neuropsychology,* *29*(1), 67–72.

Nicholson, R., & Norwood, S. (2000). The quality of forensic psychological assessments, reports, and testimony: Acknowledging the gap between promise and practice. *Law and Human Behavior, 24*(1), 9–44.

O'Connell, M. J. (2000). Prediction of return to work following traumatic brain injury: Intellectual, memory, and demographic variables. *Rehabilitation Psychology, 45*(2), 212–217.

Parry, J. W., & Drogin, E. Y. (2007). *Mental disability law, evidence and testimony: A comprehensive reference manual for lawyers, judges, and mental disability professionals.* Washington, DC: American Bar Association.

Prince, M., et al. (2007) Global mental health 1: No health without mental health. *Lancet, 370*(950), 859–877.

Randolph, C. (1998). *The repeatable battery for the assessment of neuropsychological status: Manual.* San Antonio, TX: The Psychological Corporation.

Rogers, R., Bagby, R. M., & Dickens, S. E. (1992). *Structured interview of reported symptoms (SIRS) and professional manual.* Odessa, FL: Psychological Assessment Resources.

Rogers, R., & Bender, S. (2003). Evaluation of malingering and deception. In Alan M. Goldstein (Ed.), *Handbook of psychology: Forensic psychology*, vol. 11 (pp. 109–129). Hoboken, NJ: John Wiley & Sons.

Rogers, R., & Payne, J. (2006). Damages and rewards: Assessment of malingered disorders in compensation cases. *Behavioral Sciences and the Law, 24*, 645–658.

Roh, K. S., Shin, M. S., Kim, M. S., et al. (2005). Persistent cognitive dysfunction in patients with obsessive-compulsive disorder: A naturalistic study. *Psychiatry & Clinical Neuroscience, 59*(5), 539–545.

Rorschach, H. (1921). *Psychodiagnostik* (Hans Huber Verlag, trans.). Bern, Switzerland: Bircher.

Rosen, G. (2004). Litigation and reported rates of posttraumatic stress disorder. *Personality and Individual Differences, 36*, 1291–1294.

Rosen, G., & Powel, J. (2003). Use of a symptom validity test in the forensic assessment of posttraumatic stress disorder. *Anxiety Disorders, 17*, 361–367.

Rytsaia, H., et al. (2007). Predictors of long term work disability in major depressive disorder: A prospective study. *Acta Psychiatrica Scandinavica, 115*(3), 206–213.

Samuel, R., & Mittenberg, W. (2005). Determination of malingering in disability evaluations. *Primary Psychiatry, 12*(12), 60–68.

Silverton, L., & Gruber, C. (1998). *Malingering probability scale (MPS) manual.* Los Angeles, CA: Western Psychological Services.

Social Security Administration (2002). *Annual statistical report on the Social Security disability insurance program, 2002* – Charts. Washington, DC: SSA.

Social Security Administration (2006). *Disability evaluation under Social Security (Blue Book).* SSA Pub. No. 64–039, ICN 468600, June 2006.

Souêtre, E. E. (1997). Predicting factors for absenteeism in patients with major depressive disorders. *European Journal of Epidemiology, 13*(1), 87–93.

Sreenivasan, S., Eth, S., Kirkish, P., & Garrick, T. (2003). A practical method for the evaluation of symptom exaggeration in minor head trauma among civil litigants. *Journal of the American Academy of Psychiatry and the Law, 31*(2), 220–31.

Stoddard, S., Jans, L., Ripple, J., & Kraus, L. (1998). *Chartbook on work and disability in the United States, 1998. An InfoUse Report.* Washington, DC: U.S. National Institute on Disability and Rehabilitation Research.

Stordal, K. I., et al. (2004). Impairment across executive functions in recurrent major depression. *Nordic Journal of Psychiatry, 58*(1), 41–47.

Strasberger, L., Gutheil, T., & Brodsky, A. (1997). On wearing two hats: Role conflict in serving as both psychotherapist and expert witness. *American Journal of Psychiatry, 154,* 448–456.

Sumanti, M., Boone, K., Savodnik, I., & Gorsuch, R. (2006). *Noncredible psychiatric and cognitive symptoms in a workers' compensation "stress" claim sample. Clinical Neuropsychologist, 20*(4) 754–765.

Taylor, S., Wald, J., & Asmundsom, G. (2006). Factors associated with occupational impairment in people seeking treatment for posttraumatic stress disorder. *Canadian Journal of Community Mental Health, 25*(2), 289–301.

Thompson, J. M., Gray, J. M., Hughes, J. H., Watson, S., Young, A. H., & Ferrier, I. N. (2007). Impaired working memory monitoring in euthymic bipolar patients. *Bipolar Disorders, 9*(4), 478–489.

Thoreson, R., et al. (1986). Alcoholism among psychologists: Factors in relapse and recovery. *Professional Psychology: Research and Practice, 17*(6), 497–503.

Thurman, O. (1938). The future of disability income insurance. *Journal of the American Association of University Teachers of Insurance, 5,* 59–66.

Tombaugh, T. N. (1996). *The test of memory malingering.* Toronto, Canada: Multi-Health Systems.

Tse, S., & Walsh, A. (2001). How does work work for people with bipolar disorder?. *Occupational Therapy International, 8*(3), 210–225.

U.S. Department of Health and Human Services (1999). *Mental Health: A Report of the Surgeon General.* Rockville, MD: USDHHS, Substance Abuse and Mental Health Services Administration, Center for Mental Health Services, National Institutes of Health, National Institute of Mental Health.

Victor, T. L., & Abeles, N. (2004). Coaching clients to take psychological and neuropsychological tests: A clash of ethical obligations. *Professional Psychology Research & Practice, 35*(4), 373–379.

Vore, D. A. (2007). The disability psychological independent medical evaluation. In A. Goldstein (Ed.), *Forensic psychology: Emerging topics and expanding roles* (pp. 489–510). Hoboken, NJ: John Wiley & Sons.

Wadsworth, E. J. K., Moss, S. C., Simpson, S. A., & Smith, A. P. (2005). SSRIs and cognitive performance in a working sample. *Human Psychopharmacology: Clinical & Experimental, 20,* 561–572.

Wells, K. B., Stewart, A., Hays, R. D., Burnam, A., Rogers, W., Daniels, M., et al. (1989). The functioning and well-being of depressed patients. *Journal of the American Medical Association, 262,* 914–919.

Widows, M. R., & Smith, G. P. (2005). *Structured inventory of malingered symptomatology.* Odessa, FL: Psychological Assessment Resources.

Williams, C. W., Lees-Haley, P. R., & Djanogly, S. E. (1999). Clinical scrutiny of litigants' self- reports. *Professional Psychology: Research and Practice, 30*(4), 361–367.

Williams, C. D., & Schouten, R. (2008). Assessment of occupational impairment and disability from depression. *Journal of Occupational and Environmental Medicine, 50*(4), 441–450.

Witt, P. H., & Weitz, S. E. (2007). Personal injury evaluations in motor vehicle accident cases. *Journal of Psychiatry and Law, 35,* 3–24.

World Health Organization (2001). *International classification of functioning, disability and health (ICF).* Geneva, Switzerland: World Health Organization.

World Health Organization (2002). Towards a common language for functioning, disability and health. Geneva: World Health Organization.

Tests and Specialized Tools

BDI-II: Beck Depression Inventory (Beck, 1996)

BSI: Brief Symptom Inventory (Derogatis, 1993)

CARB: Computerized Assessment of Response Bias: revised edition (Conder et al., 1997)

CLVT-II: California Verbal Learning Test—Second Edition (Delis et al., 2000)

Halstead Reitan Neuropsychological Battery (Halstead, 1947; Reitan, 1979)

M-FAST: Miller Forensic Assessment of Symptoms Test (Miller, 2005)

MMCI-III: Millon Clinical Multiaxial Inventory-III (Millon, Davis, & Millon, 1997)

MMPI-2: Minnesota Multiphasic Personality Inventory-2 (Butcher et al., 2001)

MPS: Malingering Probability Scale (Silverton & Gruger, 1998)

PAI: Personality Assessment Inventory (Morey, 2007)

PDRT: Portland Digit Recognition Test (Binder, 1993)

RBANS: Repeatable Battery for the Assessment of Neuropsychological Status (Randolph, 1998)

SCL-90-R: Symptom Checklist-90—Revised (Derogatis, 1994)

SIMS: Structured Inventory of Malingered Symptomatology (Widows & Smith, 2005)

SIRS-2: Structured Interview of Reported Symptoms, 2nd Edition (Rogers, Sewell, & Gillard, 2010)

TOMM: Test of Memory Malingering (Tombaugh, 1996)

TSI: Trauma Symptom Inventory (Briere, 1995)

VSVT: Victoria Symptom Validity Test

VIP: Validity Indicator Profile (Frederick, 1997)

WMT: Word Memory Test (Green, 2003).

References for Tests

Allen, L. M., Conder, R. L., Green, P., & Cox, D. R. (1997). *CARB'97 manual for the Computerized Assessment of Response Bias*. Durham, NC: CogniSyst.

Beck, A. T., Steer, R. A., & Brown, G. (1996). *Beck Depression Inventory manual* (2nd ed.). San Antonio, TX: Psychological Corporation.

Binder, L.R. (1993). *Portland Digit Recognition Test Manual,* 2nd Ed. Beaverton, OR: Author

Briere, J. (1995). *Trauma Symptom Inventory professional manual*. Odessa, FL: Psychological Assessment Resources.

Butcher, J. N., Graham, J. R., Ben-Porath, Y. S., Tellegen, A., Dahlstrom, W. G., & Kaemmer, B. (2001). *MMPI-2: Manual for administration and scoring* (rev. ed.). Minneapolis: University of Minnesota Press.

Delis, D.C., Kramer, J.H., Kaplan, E., & Ober, B.A. (2000). California Verbal Learning Test: Second Edition. San Antonio, TX: Psychological Corporation.

Derogatis, L.R.(1993). *BSI Brief Symptom Inventory: Administration, Scoring, and Procedure Manual* (4th Ed.). Minneapolis, MN: National Computer Systems.

Derogatis, L. R. 1994 SCL-90-R: Administration, Scoring and Procedures Manual. National Computer Systems, Inc., Minneapolis.

Frederick, R. I. (1997). *Validity Indicator Profile manual*. Minnetonka, MN: NCS Assessments.

Green P. Manual for the *Word Memory Test for Windows*. Edmonton: Green's Publishing; 2003.

Miller, H. A. (2001). *M-FAST: Miller-Forensic Assessment of Symptoms Test professional manual*. Odessa, FL: Psychological Assessment Resources.

Millon, T., Davis, R., & Millon, C. (1997). *Millon Clinical Multiaxial Inventory-III manual* (2nd ed.). Minneapolis, MN: National Computer Systems.

Morey, L. C. (1991). *The Personality Assessment Inventory: Professional manual*. Odessa, FL: Psychological Assessment Resources.

Randolph, C. (1998). *The Repeatable Battery for the Assessment of Neuropsychological Status: Manual*. San Antonio, TX: The Psychological Corporation.

Reitan, R. M. (1979). *Manual for administration of neuropsychological test batteries for adults and children*. Tuscon, AZ: Author.

Rogers, R., Sewell, K., & Gillard, N. (2010). *Structured Interview of Reported Symptoms professional manual* (2nd ed.) (SIRS-2). Odessa, FL: Psychological Assessment Resources.

Silverton, L., & Gruber, C. (1998). *Malingering Probability Scale (MPS) manual*. Los Angeles, CA: Western Psychological Services.

Tombaugh, T. N. (1996). *Test of Memory Malingering*. Toronto, Ontario: MultiHealth Systems.

Widows, M. R., & Smith, G. P. (2005). *Structured Inventory of Malingered Symptomatology professional manual*. Odessa, FL: Psychological Assessment Resources, 2005.

Cases and Statutes

Americans with Disabilities Act, 42 U.S.C., Sec. 12101 (1990).

Berkshire Life Insurance Company v. Adelberg, 698 So. 2d 828 (Fla. 1997).

Black & Decker Disability Plan v. Nord, 538 U.S. 822 (2003).

Bowen v. Yuckert, 482 U.S. 137 (1987).

Brosnan v. Provident Life & Accident Insurance Company (E.D. Pa. 1998).

Code of Federal Regulations (20 C.F.R. §§ 404.1500-404.1599).

Damascus v. Provident Life and Accident Insurance Company, 933 F. Supp. 885, (N.D. Cal. 1996).

Emerson v. Fireman's Fund, American Life Insurance Company, 524 F. Supp. 1262 (N.D. Ga. 1981).

The Employee Retirement Income Security Act of 1974 (ERISA).

Federal Employers Liability Act (FELA), 45 U.S.C. § 51 et seq. (1908)

Firestone Tire & Rubber Company V. Bruch, 489 U.S. 101 (1989).

Gates v. The Prudential Insurance Company of America, 240 A. D. 444, 270 N.Y.S. 282 (App. Div. 1934).

Goomar v. Centennial Life Insurance Company, 855 F. Supp. 319, U.S. Dist. Cal. 1994.

Grayboyes v. General American Life Insurance Company,1995 U.S. Dist. LEXIS 4233 (E.D. Pa. 1995).

Hangarter v. Provident Life and Accident Insurance Company & The Paul Revere Life Insurance Company; UNUM Provident Corporation, 373 F.3rd 998 (2004); U.S. App. LEXIS 12841 (2004).

Heckler v. Campbell, 461 U.S. 458 (1983).

Holzer v. MBL Life Assurance Corporation, 1999 U.S. Dist. LEXIS 13094, 1999 WL 649004 (S.D.N.Y.).

The Individuals with Disabilities Education Improvement Act of 2004 (IDEA).

Kupshik v. John Hancock Mutual Life Insurance Company, 1:98-CV-3-CAM (M.D. Ga., 2000).

Lasser v. Reliance Standard Life Insurance Company, 2003 U.S. App. LEXIS 19345 (3d Cir. 2003).

Laucks v. Provident Companies, et al., 97-CV-1507, M.D. PA, 1999 WL 33320463 (M.D. PA.).

Massachusetts Mutual Life Insurance Company v. Jefferson, 104 S.W.3d 13 (Tenn. Ct. App. 2002).

Massachusetts Mutual Life Insurance Company v. Ouellette, 159 Vt. 187, 617 A. 2d 132 (1992).

McCarran-Ferguson Act (15 U.S.C. § 6701).

Metropolitan Life Insurance Company et al. v. Glenn, 554 U.S.06-923(2008).

Pilot Life Insurance Company v. Dedeaux, 481 U.S. 41 (1987).

Social Security Act (42 U.S.C. § 423).

United States Code (28 U.S.C.A.§1332).

Key Terms

Abuse of discretion: A failure to properly consider the facts or apply the appropriate procedures in the denial of a claim, resulting in a finding that the denial was "arbitrary and capricious."

Arbitrary and capricious standard: A determination that there was not a rational basis for the denial of a claim. Related to "abuse of discretion."

Attending physician: The professional treating the claimant for the condition related to the disability.

Bad faith: The intentional or malicious failure to abide by the terms of a contract.

De novo standard: A determination that the court will set aside the original claim decision and make its own decision based on a fresh review of the evidence.

Disability: The legal determination of the claimant's eligibility for benefits.

Dissimulation: The intentional misrepresentation of the nature or severity of one's symptoms.

ERISA (Employee Retirement Security Act of 1974): Federal legislation that regulates the operation of employer-provided health benefit plans, including group disability insurance.

Factual disability: Impairments resulting from an illness or injury that prevent or limit the claimant's ability to perform his or her occupational duties (compare to "legal disability").

Functional capacity: What an individual can do or accomplish, as well as the knowledge, understanding, or beliefs that may be necessary for such accomplishment.

Group disability insurance: Provided by an employer as part of an employee's health care benefits.

Impairment: The loss of function due to a health condition, disorder, or disease.

Independent medical examination (IME): An evaluation obtained from a licensed psychologist or psychiatrist, who is independent from both the insurance company and the claimant, to provide information relevant to determining the claimant's eligibility for disability benefits.

Individual disability insurance (IDI): A disability insurance policy purchased by an individual (often by those who are self-employed) separate from and unrelated to benefits provided by an employer.

Legal disability: The claimant is unable to work due to legal restrictions, such as the loss of a professional license or incarceration (compare to "factual disability").

Risk of relapse claim: A claim for disability benefits made when the claimant has recovered or whose symptoms are in remission, who contends that returning to work would result in a relapse or exacerbation of symptoms.

Situational factors: Factors unrelated to a clinical condition that affect the claimant's work capacity.

Social Security disability insurance (SSDI): A U.S. government federal insurance program, funded by payroll taxes, designed to provide income to people who are unable to work because of a disability.

Substantial and material duties: The core, essential duties of a job that are vital to its performance.

Substantial gainful activity (SGA): Monthly earnings above an established threshold; used in Social Security disability cases to determine eligibility for benefits when a claimant is working.

Treating physician rule: In Social Security disability claims, the opinion of the treating physician, if well supported by medical and other substantial evidence, is entitled to more weight than other factors, such as the opinions of consultants or examining physicians.

Work capacity: The claimant's ability to function in his or her occupation.

Index

About the Author

Lisa Drago Piechowski, Ph.D., is a forensic psychologist in independent practice specializing in issues related to disability, fitness for duty, worker's compensation, and other employment-related matters. In addition to performing assessments, Dr. Piechowski serves as a consultant to insurance companies, attorneys, and employers. She is the author of book chapters and articles on disability evaluation and consultation, fitness-for-duty evaluations, and Americans with Disabilities Act evaluations and is a frequent presenter of continuing education workshops for psychologists and attorneys. She has served on the executive board of the American Academy of Forensic Psychology and is co-chair of its Continuing Education committee. She is a member of the examination faculty of the American Board of Forensic Psychology. She is the former chair of the American Psychological Association Committee on Professional Practice and Standards and is a member of the APA Office of the General Counsel Committee on Legal Issues. She served on the Taskforce for the Revision of the Specialty Guidelines for Forensic Psychology.

Dr. Piechowski is board-certified in forensic psychology by the American Board of Professional Psychology.